Arguments for a
Non-transformational
Grammar

Arguments for a Non-transformational Grammar

Richard A. Hudson

The University of Chicago Press

Chicago and London

The University of Chicago Press, Chicago 60637
The University of Chicago Press, Ltd., London

© 1976 by The University of Chicago
All rights reserved. Published 1976
Printed in the United States of America

80 79 78 77 76   9 8 7 6 5 4 3 2 1

Library of Congress Cataloging in Publication Data

Hudson, R. A.
    Arguments for a non-transformational grammar.

    Bibliography: p.
    Includes index.
    1.   Grammar, Comparative and general.   2.   Gener-
ative grammar.   I.   Title.
P151.H8   415   76–604
ISBN 0–226–35799–6

Richard A. Hudson was graduated from Cambridge University and
received his Ph.D. at the School of Oriental and African Studies at the
University of London. He now teaches in the Department of Phonetics and
Linguistics at University College, London. He is the author of *English
Complex Sentences: An Introduction to Systemic Grammar* (1971).

To Gay and Lucy

Contents

Preface

This book is an attempt to justify an alternative to transformational-generative grammar, called 'daughter-dependency' grammar, which is better at doing the things transformationalists want to do, but can do them without the use of either transformations or the deep/surface distinction in syntax. Since much of it is taken up with criticisms of transformational grammar, I should like to emphasize here that I think very highly indeed of very many proponents of this theory—I do not believe that people who accept false theories do so because they are fools. Indeed, I should be proud to be ranked with most of the transformational linguists whose works I refer to in this book. There is certainly no way in which this book could have been written—or daughter-dependency theory developed—without the stimulus and ideas that have come out of the transformational-generative school. I should like to record my particular debt to my transformational colleagues, from whom I have learned a lot—including the very general point that one is much more likely to persuade a transformational linguist if one plays the game according to his rules.

My other obvious source of ideas is Michael Halliday. Daughter-dependency theory is a rather radical version of 'systemic' theory, and all versions of systemic theory derive ultimately from Halliday's article 'Categories of the theory of grammar' of 1961. However, I have also benefited from working and talking with other linguists interested in these theories, including all those at the 'Systemic grammar workshops' of 1974 and 1975, and some with whom I've had more or less extensive correspondence—especially Michael McCord, Joe Taglicht, Jim Martin and Robin Fawcett.

I am most grateful for the comments I have received on earlier versions of this book from Paul Schachter and an anonymous reader, who both went to great trouble to point out shortcomings in content and presentation, and I think there is hardly a single point that they made which hasn't led to some improvement in the text. I also had extensive comments from Keith Brown, Gerald Gazdar, Anita Hochster, Grover Hudson, Mike Lucas, John Lyons, Michael McCord, Jim Martin, Joe Taglicht and David Young; and I am grateful to all of them for their trouble.

Various suggestions made by students attending my classes on the theory will be found in the text, and are gratefully acknowledged.

Finally, a big thank you to my wife Gay for putting up with a clattering typewriter and an absent-minded husband the past year, and for all the encouragement she has given me.

University College, London

1 Introduction

1.1. Transformational Grammar and Daughter-dependency Grammar

In every introductory book on transformational-generative syntax, there is an argument for the necessity of transformations that runs something like this: let us assume that the syntactic structure of a sentence should be represented as a labeled bracketing of a string of formatives (or by the theoretically equivalent 'phrase-marker'). Now the obvious way to generate structural representations of this kind is by means of 'phrase-structure' rules. But it can be shown that phrase-structure rules do the job badly, since there are many types of structural relation that they can show only clumsily, if at all. Therefore phrase-structure rules need to be supplemented by some more powerful type of rule to match the kind of structure phrase-structure rules *can* generate onto the kind we actually need to represent surface structures. Rules of this kind are transformations. Therefore transformations are necessary in the generation of syntactic structures. And because transformations are needed, there must be at least two distinct structural representations for the syntax of any sentence, one to act as input and the other to act as output of the transformations—i.e. there is a difference between deep structure and surface structure.

Haas (1973: 102) summarizes the argument pithily: 'No-one will deny that "Immediate Constituent" analysis of the familiar sort is crude and superficial. But current models of generative grammar have incorporated it. I.C. analysis is considered to be, on the whole, UNCONTROVERSIAL as well as INADEQUATE. Since it is accepted as uncontroversial, its inadequacy is to be cured by supplementation, rather than revision: something "deeper" being added to redeem it.' If you accept the intial assumption, it is hard to disagree with the conclusion: transformations and the deep/surface structure contrast *are* needed; and since transformational-generative grammar, in its various versions, seems to give the best account of these concepts, it must, to that extent, be the best model of syntactic structure.

But what if you don't accept the initial assumption? Clearly, the chain of arguments collapses: if syntactic structures aren't best represented as a labeled bracketing, then phrase-structure rules may not be relevant in generating them, and whatever types of rule are needed may not have the same limitations as phrase-structure rules, so there may be no need to include transforma-tions among the rules; and if there are no transformations, it could be that there is no basis for distinguishing between deep and sur-face syntactic structures. Of course, simply rejecting the initial assumption doesn't *in itself* lead to the ultimate rejection of trans-formations and the deep/surface contrast; it could be that even a different type of structural representation would turn out to be difficult or impossible to generate without recourse to transforma-tions. But at least it should be clear that rejecting the initial as-sumption would make it necessary to work out a new set of argu-ments for transformations.

What I shall try to do in this book is show the advantages of assuming that syntactic structures, as generated by a grammar, should be different from those generated by a transformational grammar—to anticipate, I shall favor structures more like (*a*) than (*b*) (a phrase-marker), for a sentence like 'The farmer killed the duckling' (see fig. 1).

To support this claim, I shall show that structures of this type can be generated, though by means of rules that include neither phrase-structure rules nor transformations. Moreover, I shall be able to point to a number of weaknesses in transformational grammars which are not found in grammars of the type I shall be describing.

We shall need to refer to this theory, and I propose to call it 'daughter-dependency syntax'. It can be thought of as a version of 'systemic grammar' (see the references in Hudson 1971 and,

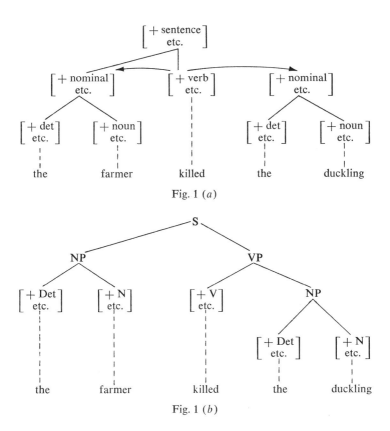

Fig. 1 (*a*)

Fig. 1 (*b*)

more recently, Berry 1975), but the name 'systemic' doesn't seem very helpful, since I have abandoned the term 'system' on which it is based, preferring to use the more self-explanatory term "classification rule' (see chapter 2). 'Daughter-dependency' has the advantage of emphasizing the fact that this model represents a combination of the properties of American-style constituency grammar (as in American 'structuralism' and transformational grammar) with those of European-style dependency grammar. The 'dependency' part shows the latter alignment directly, but the 'daughter' part is meant to show the former alignment, since dependency grammar proper allows only *sisters* (more precisely, words or morphemes) to show dependency relations, and the concept of 'daughters' makes sense only if one accepts that smaller items are 'part of' some larger item (phrase or sentence) which operates as a single unit. Besides, there is an important kind of rule in this grammar called a 'daughter-dependency' rule (for introducing dependent daughters), which plays an essential role in the generation of structures, so no great harm will have been done if this model gets thought of as 'the model that has daughter-dependency rules', as the transformational model is associated with transformational rules. There is a brief discussion of the relations between this model and dependency grammars in Appendix 2. (An alternative name, suggested by Michael McCord, is 'unistructural syntax'; some readers may feel this is a better name, as it highlights the fact that such grammars fit all the syntactic information about a sentence into a single, integrated structure, as we shall see in 1.2.3 below.)

1.2. A First Sketch of Daughter-dependency Syntax

Just as a transformational grammar includes rules of a number of different types (phrase-structure rules, lexical-insertion rules, transformational rules, lexical-redundancy rules, output constraints), so does a daughter-dependency grammar. The next chapter will discuss the various types of rule in some detail, so here all we need do is give a very rough picture of what they are like and how they interact with one another in the derivation of a sentence's syntactic structure.

1.2.1. *Levels of Language*

Before introducing the rule-types, I ought to deal with a couple of preliminary matters. The first is the relation between syntax and the other levels of linguistic structure—phonology and semantics, in particular. The assumption on which daughter-dependency syntax is based is that syntax is separate from both these other levels, and has its own, autonomous set of rules, which allow one to predict which sentences will be *syntactically* well-formed and

and which won't. This immediately distinguishes daughter-dependency grammar from any version of 'generative semantics', since in the latter it is assumed that there is just one level, of 'semantic syntax', and therefore no distinction in principle between syntactic and semantic well-formedness, although deviance may be of a relatively 'surface' kind (e.g. *'Who do you think that came?') or a relatively 'deep' kind (e.g. *'a pregnant bachelor'). To give a full set of arguments in favor of autonomous syntax would take us too far from the main theme of the book (the relation between daughter-dependency and transformational grammar in general), but I might mention just two kinds of factor that encourage me to believe that generative semantics is wrong.

First, how can generative semantics handle idioms like 'pull X's leg', meaning 'tease X'? It is easy to show that the *syntactic* structure of 'He pulled her leg' is the same, whether it has its literal or its idiomatic meaning, at least if one considers surface structure and the possibility of applying transformations such as passive ('Her leg is always being pulled'). And yet the literal and idiomatic meanings have virtually nothing in common—indeed, we can presumably take it that the idiomatic meaning will be represented in the same way, bar a few details, as the ordinary meaning of 'tease X'. So the problem for generative semantics is how to get from a semantic representation suitable for 'He teased her', to a syntactic representation suitable for 'He pulled her leg', and to do so moreover before transformations like passivization can apply. The main argument for generative semantics is that the transformations needed for syntax (i.e. for relating surface structures to 'deep' structures) will in fact take you right through to the semantic structure (with the help of a handful of extra rules). But surely idioms are clear cases where this is not so: the relation between the semantic and syntactic structures of 'He pulled her leg', in its idiomatic sense, is quite different from any relation handled by 'ordinary' syntactic rules. They are much more like the arbitrary relations stated in the lexicon—which, it should be noticed, are relations between structures on one level and structures on a different level, as between sound and meaning in any morpheme. Until there is more evidence than what is presently available (e.g. Newmeyer 1972) that generative semantics can handle idioms, they must stand as evidence in favor of a separation of syntax and semantics.

A second reason for believing in the separation of syntax from semantics, as autonomous levels, is that the same phenomena can require different classifications on the two levels. The clearest instance of this that I know of is number in the noun-phrase. The argument runs as follows: there are some noun-phrases (or nouns —it makes no difference to the argument) which are syntactically plural but not semantically plural (such as *these bathroom scales,* which may be ambiguous semantically but in one of its readings must be as singular semantically as, say, *this bathroom weighing-machine;* cf. also *these oats* versus *this wheat*); and there are others which are semantically plural but not syntactically plural, notably the following two cases. First, there are noun-phrases with collective heads, such as *the committee,* which can occur with verbs like *disperse* which need to be marked as occurring only with subjects that refer to a group of individuals—i.e. semantically plural subjects; and second, there are noun-phrases with heads like *heap,* as in *a large heap of logs,* which can occur in a reciprocal construction ('A large heap of logs were piled on top of each other'), in contrast with *a large heap of sand,* which has to be semantically singular. I take it as axiomatic that this kind of situation requires two different levels, each with its own classification of the items concerned.

It might be thought that in a transformational approach the problem could be solved without postulating separate levels of semantics and syntax, simply by having some kind of rule for changing features between the deepest representations (which would show semantic number) and the more surface ones (which would show syntactic number). However, this would then raise a separate problem, namely that a later rule (the rule for subject-verb concord) would need to be able to refer to the semantic classification, which would make it a global rule (i.e. a rule which has to refer both to the structures on which it operates and also to a structure at some earlier stage in the derivation;

Lakoff (1970*a*)). This is so because, so far as I can see, the proper formulation of subject-verb concord in English is that the verb shows plural concord (i.e. lacks *-s*) if the subject is either syntactically or semantically plural. To this part of the argument it could be replied that there is good evidence that global rules are needed in any case, so showing that this rule is global proves nothing. On the other hand, this reply carries weight only to the extent that it is *possible* to formulate global rules in a transformational grammar, which I shall argue later it isn't, since there is no natural way in which a noun-phrase node in one structure can be identified with a noun-phrase node in some other structure in the same derivation. If the two nodes are in different levels of representation, on the other hand, they will be connected by the realization rules (or interpretation rules) that relate the two levels, so the subject-verb concord rule could be formulated.

Readers who think that there is more to be gained from merging syntax and semantics than from keeping them separate aren't likely to have been convinced just by these two arguments, but with apologies I must leave it at that, as far as the present book is concerned; considering the amount of ink that has gone into the controversy within transformational grammar already, it would be surprising if one could find any knock-down arguments. Readers who like generative semantics are likely to object to some of the analyses we shall discuss below on the grounds that they don't reflect semantic relations sufficiently clearly or directly. To this the reply has to be, first, that this is what happens when you separate syntax from semantics, whether in transformational or daughter-dependency grammar, and second, that the extent to which the syntactic analyses *do* reflect meaning is impressive, considering that they aren't *required* to do so by the rules of the game. After all, it is only if you start from the assumption that syntax and semantics are separate that you can really find out how closely they are related, and be impressed by the many points at which they are in almost a one–one relationship. (It might be worth mentioning that there are advocates of 'systemic grammar' too who favor a generative-semantics position, notably Fawcett 1974.)

To return to the general question of the relations among the levels, then, we shall be viewing syntax as an autonomous level (as in Chomskyan 'interpretive semantics'). However, unlike Chomsky I see no reason to think that there should be only *one* level of language that is autonomous, so I shouldn't be at all surprised if others more competent than myself could show that semantics and phonology are both autonomous as well. Whether or not this is so is a question that can be left open, and won't affect the arguments in the rest of the book.

There remain two other questions about levels of language: where does the lexicon fit in, and is there a level of morphology? On the question of the *lexicon,* there is no great difference of principle between daughter-dependency and transformational grammars: in both, the lexicon is a list of separate items, each of which brings together syntactic, semantic and phonological information about one morpheme (or idiomatic string of morphemes). Whenever a syntactic structure offers an environment into which the syntactic part of a lexical entry says that it can be fitted, it may be inserted; but for most syntactic environments there are a large number of lexical items which could be inserted, the only differences among the lexical items being in their meaning and pronunciation, and not in their syntax. It should be remarked, however, that there are versions of systemic grammar in which lexical differences, such as that between *apple* and *pear,* are treated as 'most delicate grammar', meaning that they would be distinguished syntactically; see for example Halliday in Parret (1974: 90). It is hard to reconcile this view with the view that lexical and grammatical items need not be coextensive—that idioms, for instance, can cut across the segmentation needed for syntax; see Halliday (1961: 273).

There is an important difference, however, between the effects of inserting a lexical item in daughter-dependency and transformational grammars, at least of the *Aspects* type: in the latter, when a lexical item is inserted (in deep structure), the result is that the *whole* content of the lexical item is inserted, including its meaning and its pronunciation, into the same structure, with the result that deep structures contain semantic and phonological features as well as strictly syntactic features. In daughter-dependency grammar, on the other hand, the lexicon is seen as a (very large) set of interlevel rules, defining possible relations among the three levels of semantics, syntax and phonology, so lexical insertion involves finding a lexical entry which is compatible with the syntactic environment, and then inserting its meaning into the semantic structure and its pronunciation into the phonological structure. Better still (see 1.2.2), lexical items in daughter-dependency can be seen as well-formedness conditions on the meanings and pronunciations that can correspond to particular syntactic environments. In this way daughter-dependency avoids mixing up semantic and phonological information with the syntactic structure, as happens in the *Aspects* type of transformational grammars. It should be pointed out, incidentally, that in the transformational approach there is nothing to prevent all the semantic features belonging to a lexical item from being carried through from the deep structure to the surface structure, so that we find phonological features in deep structure, where they're not wanted, and semantic features in surface structures, where they weren't originally wanted (although they *will* be needed there if all semantic interpretation rules are to apply to surface structure, as Chomsky suggests now—see Chomsky 1974—so for the more recent version of transformational grammar, the only problem is the presence of phonological features in deep structure).

Another difference between the roles of the lexicon in daughter-dependency and transformational grammar is that in daughter-dependency grammars the lexicon doesn't contain any syntactic information which isn't already present in the structure into which it is inserted (nothing, in other words, corresponding to Lakoff's 'rule features'; Lakoff 1970*b*). From this it follows that no syntactic rules presuppose that lexical insertion has already taken place, so that lexical insertion can wait until the whole syntactic structure for the sentence has been built up—or, in terms of well-formedness conditions, lexical well-formedness can be kept separate from syntactic well-formedness. In a transformational grammar, on the other hand, lexical insertion is generally assumed to take place either between the phrase-structure rules and the transformations (Chomsky 1965) or among the transformations (McCawley 1968*a*)—although it is interesting to note a suggestion that lexical insertion might be better located at shallow structure (Hochster 1974), which perhaps could be reconciled fairly easily with insertion in surface structure, which corresponds to the position taken in daughter-dependency grammar.

The last question about levels is whether or not there should be a separate level of *morphology*. This is an extremely complicated question, but the balance of evidence does seem to be in favor of distinguishing morphology in some way from the rest of the grammar. For instance, there are cases where the morphological and syntactic analyses of words conflict—for example, in Latin there are verbs which are traditionally said to be 'passive in form (sc. morphology) and active in meaning (sc. syntax)', such as *conor* 'I try'; and there are systematic differences among words that have everything to do with their morphology and nothing to do with their syntactic similarities and differences (e.g. strong vs weak verbs in English; declension classes of nouns in Latin; *-er* vs *-ir* vs *-re* verbs in French; and so on). At least in cases like this, it seems clear that the syntax should have nothing to say about the formal similarities and differences among words, but should simply specify their syntactic properties, using syntactic features. It seems equally clear that the rules needed for generating inflectional paradigms aren't phonological rules, since the differences in form that have to be described are often completely arbitrary from a phonological point of view. Therefore, if inflectional paradigms are to be generated, they must be generated by a separate set of rules from both syntax and phonology—namely, a set of morphological rules. Whether or not the same is true of *derivational* paradigms I very much doubt, pace Halle (1973), but this is an even more complicated question, and we can fortunately leave it open, as far as the rest of this book is concerned. Moreover we can even assume, for simplicity, that morphology is the name of a separate component but not of a separate level (that is, it simply relates the level of syntax—and probably also semantics—to the level of phonology, without generating an extra level of structure in between). On this assumption, there are still just three levels: semantics, syntax and phonology.

To summarize, the relation between syntax and other levels and 'components' is assumed to be like Fig. 2.

levels	components	
semantic level	autonomous (?) rules for generating semantic structures	
	rules mapping syntactic and semantic structures onto one another	lexical items mapping phonological, syntactic and semantic properties onto one another
syntactic level	autonomous rules for generating syntactic structures	
	rules mapping syntactic and phonological structures onto one another (including morphological rules)	
phonological level	autonomous (?) rules for generating phonological structures	

Fig. 2

In this book, we shall be concerned with only two of the components—the 'autonomous rules for generating syntactic structures', or *syntactic rules,* and the 'lexical items mapping phonological, syntactic and semantic properties onto one another', or *lexicon.* Moreover, we shall be concerned with only the one level, of *syntax,* so the lexicon will be discussed only with reference to the specifically *syntactic* properties of the items that it contains.

1.2.2. *Rules, Conditions and Processes*

Rules in a generative grammar can be seen, and are seen, in either of two ways: either as *conditions* that a structure has to satisfy in order to count as well-formed ('well-formedness conditions'; McCawley 1968*b*), or as *operations* that must have been executed in building up the structure from nothing if it is to count as well-formed. In a transformational grammar of the more conservative type, as described in *Aspects of the Theory of Syntax,* for instance (Chomsky 1965), phrase-structure rules and transformations are seen as operations that have to have been executed, whereas output constraints and relations between the separate parts of a lexical entry are seen as conditions (though this term has never been used, so far as I know, of lexical items).

The main difference between operations and conditions seems to be simply a matter of terminology—how you translate the rule into ordinary language, in fact: do you translate it in 'dynamic' terms, as an 'instruction' to 'do' something, or do you translate it in 'static' terms, as a relation that has to hold (or may hold) between elements? When Chomsky talks about 'rewrite' rules, it is easiest to interpret him 'dynamically', and to think of the main types of rewrite rules (phrase-structure rules) as though they were defining operations; but when he says that structures mustn't contain internal sentence boundaries if they are to count as well-formed surface structures, one tends to interpret him 'statically', in terms of conditions on well-formedness. On the other hand, it's not too difficult to rethink the interpretations, so that you see re-write rules as conditions on well-formedness, and output conditions and relations within the lexicon as operations—indeed, all of these possibilities have actually been realized in recent years (e.g. McCawley 1968*b,* and Lakoff 1971, suggest that rewrite rules could be seen as conditions on well-formedness; Chomsky 1972: 132 sees output constraints as rules for assigning asterisks, by an operation of asterisk-addition; and McCawley 1968*a,* and all other literature on 'prelexical syntax', see relations between meanings and forms in the lexicon as transformations, replacing one by the other).

It is at least possible, then, that there isn't a substantive issue here at all. In general, any rule can be seen in either way, and neither the content of the grammar nor its output will be affected. However, there is an important difference between conditions and operations which I believe has never been commented on before: it is a question of how they handle 'free' (i.e. syntactically unrestricted) order of elements, such as the position of many kinds of adverbial in English, or the order of elements in languages with 'free word-order'. If it could be established empirically in some way (by psycholinguistic experiment, I assume) that free order of elements is more natural or simple than fixed order, or if the converse could be established, then we should want it to be easier for a grammar to allow the more natural type of structure (be it the one with fixed or the one with free order) than to allow the other one. So far as I know, there is no empirical evidence either way at present, but it is at least conceivable that there could be, so let us assume, for the sake of argument, that it had been shown that fixed order is less natural than free order. Now let us turn to the form of ordering rules in a grammar, and assume they take the form 'If there is an X and a Y, then X must precede Y' (this is the form of the sequence rules in a daughter-dependency grammar—see 3.7—but it is more or less the same as the 'ordering' aspect of phrase-structure rules too). We can now take these two assumptions and put them together, and draw the conclusion that sequence rules should be taken as conditions on well-formedness rather than as operations: as conditions, a case of free order is handled simply by not having any rule at all, since there will be no order that needs to be ruled out. In contrast, if rules are seen as operations, then it becomes necessary to define a separate sequencing operation for each of the possible orders of elements. If, on the other hand, the facts turned out to be the reverse of what we assumed above—if it turned out, that is, that free order were less natural than fixed order—then clearly this argument for taking rules as conditions would collapse (though I don't think any facts would support the rules-as-operations approach more than the rule-as-conditions approach).

The reason for raising the question of conditions and processes here is to prepare the reader for daughter-dependency syntax, in which it probably makes more sense to interpret the rules as conditions rather than as operations—in contrast with transformational grammar, where it is probably the other way around. Rules of one type, at least (the classification rules) have to be taken as a set of conditions, in order for their interaction with the rest of the grammar to make any sense; but there are others that can be taken as operations, as in transformations. The big difference from transformational grammar, though, is that in daughter-dependency syntax the rules that have to be taken as conditions on well-formedness are at the heart of the grammar, and are, para-doxically, the 'creative' part of it, in that they provide the input to the other rules; whereas in transformational grammar they are more peripheral.

Wherever there is a danger of the reader being confused or misled over the way to interpret rules in daughter-dependency grammar, it will be helpful to come back to the question of con-ditions and operations. In most cases it will make little difference whether he takes the rules as conditions or operations, and I shall take advantage of this ambiguity in discussing the rules—some-times it is simply easier to talk about them as though they were operations.

1.2.3. *What a Daughter-dependency Grammar Generates*

The most important fact about the structural descriptions gen-erated by a daughter-dependency grammar is that only *one* such description is generated per sentence (except, of course, in the case of sentences that are syntactically ambiguous). There is nothing to match the transformational distinction between deep and surface structures within syntax: the one structural descrip-tion contains all the syntactic facts about the sentence, from those that would be shown by a transformational deep structure to those that would belong in a transformational surface structure. The single syntactic structure of daughter-dependency grammar has to be sufficiently 'deep' to be reasonably easy to relate to its meaning, but also 'surface' enough to map onto phonological structure. To take a single example: for a sentence like 'What do you think happened?', it generates a structure which has all the words in their surface order (i.e. *what* before *do,* and so on), but which also shows that *what* is subject of *happened* rather than of *think*.

A second fact is one that has already been hinted at: the struc-tures that a daughter-dependency grammar generates are not equivalent to labeled, bracketed strings, as transformational phrase-markers are. There are two reasons for this. First, one node may be connected 'upward' to more than one higher node —for instance, in the example just given, the node corresponding to *what* would be connected upward both to the node right at the top (corresponding to the main clause: an interrogative clause, with *what* as its wh-item) and to the node corresponding to the embedded clause, whose verb is *happened* and whose subject is *what* (see fig. 3).

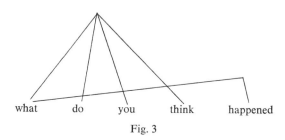

what   do   you   think   happened

Fig. 3

The second reason is that nodes can be connected to the rest of the structure not only upward and downward, as in a phrase-marker, but also *sideways*. For example, all the noun-phrases with reference to which a verb would be 'strictly subcategorized' in a Fillmorean transformational grammar (Fillmore 1968) are linked to the verb in a daughter-dependency structure. This means that there are lines in the structural diagram linking the verb to subjects, objects, predicative complements, and so on, as well as any lines that may link these noun-phrases upward to a higher node. Since there is no sense in which the subject, say, can be said to be 'part' of the verb, or vice versa, these links are different from those shown in a transformational phrase-structure tree, which all connect parts ('daughters') to wholes ('mothers'). The daughter-dependency diagram for 'What do you think happened?' (fig. 4) will have at least three sideways links, between 'sisters': one connecting *you* to *think,* and another connecting *what* to *happened;* a third link connects *think* to the whole of the clause consisting of *what* and *happened,* its 'complement'. (*Think* and *what happened* are sisters in that both are part of the same whole, namely, the whole sentence; so both are also daughters of this sentence, although only *think* has a daughter-dependency link to the top node: the presence of *think* depends on features of the

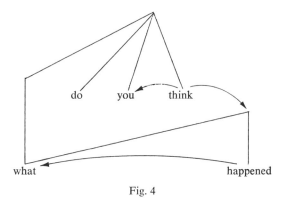

Fig. 4

mother, but that of *what happened* depends on features of *think*.)
The sideways lines have arrows at one end, to show the direction
in which dependence goes: the complement depends on the verb,
rather than vice versa. This will be explained more fully in the
next section.

A third fact about daughter-dependency structure diagrams
(which, incidentally, can be called 'trees' only by a stretch of the
imagination) is that they have syntactic features attached to *all*
nodes, and not just to the bottom nodes, as in transformational
phrase-markers (we shall return to Chomsky's suggested changes
in this respect in the next paragraph). In transformational grammars, formatives can be cross-classified, by having a number of
different features attached to the same node; but in a daughter-
dependency grammar *all* syntactic constituents, of *any* size (from
the whole sentence down) can be, and are, cross-classified in this
way—for instance, features attached to the top node in the diagram for 'What do you think happened?' show that it is interrogative and that it is a main clause—in contrast with *what . . .
happened,* which is neither interrogative nor main, and with,
say, '(I'd like to know) what you think happened', which is
interrogative but not main. If we pretend, for the sake of simplicity, that these relationships are shown by the features [± in-
terrogative] and [± main], the diagram (see fig. 5) starts to look
more like the kind of daughter-dependency diagram we shall be
discussing later in this book.

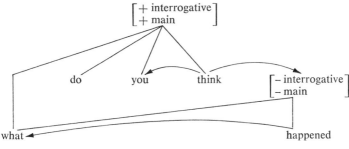

Fig. 5

(The simplification comes in the feature [± main], which won't appear at all in our proposed grammar.)

Having features on higher nodes as well as on lower ones means that 'categories', in the Chomskyan sense (i.e. S, NP, VP, V, etc.), can be treated simply as features—in fact, we shall include the features [± sentence], [± nominal] and [± verb], among the features in our grammar. Chomsky suggested some years ago that the distinction between features and categories might be abandoned (1970: 208), but his suggestion seems to have had no impact on transformational linguistics at all—at least, not on published analyses. The reason that this should be so is easy to see: it is impossible to expand a bundle of features by means of phrase-structure rules (which must, of course, have been the reason for the original principle that features should be attached only to terminal nodes—they couldn't have been attached anywhere else, given the generative apparatus available). For instance, how could phrase-structure rules expand a bundle of features like [+ interrogative, + main]? If there were a rule whose input was the *whole* of this bundle, it would miss generalizations about the reflexes of the features in it taken individually; but if there were a separate rule expanding each feature, how should their outputs be integrated with one another, given that they each define properties of the *same* sentence? It is hardly surprising that very few published analyses actually assign features to higher nodes (cf. for example Dougherty 1970), and that *none* (that I know of) attempt to write phrase-structure rules (but see Anderson, 1971: 23 for a partial attempt to do so within a rather different model).

One final fact about daughter-dependency structures is worth noting: some nodes (but not all) have *function*-labels attached to them, whose role is simply to help in the left-to-right ordering of constituents. (As we shall see in 3.5, their formal properties are quite different from those of features, and there is no question of their being fitted into the classification rules, along with the features.) There are just four or five functions relevant to the structure of the sentence, and probably another four or five that are relevant to that of the noun-phrase; in both cases, the functions, like features, can occur in bundles—i.e. with more than one attached to a single node. In 'What do you think happened?', *what* has the function TOPIC, as far as the main clause is concerned, and both SUBJECT and TOPIC as far as the embedded clause is concerned, and *you* just has the function SUBJECT.

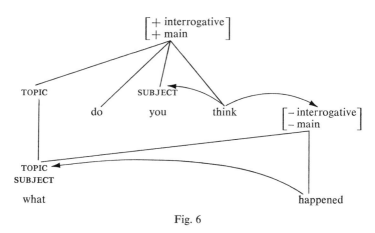

Fig. 6

Fig. 6 illustrates all the main characteristics of a daughter-dependency structure—the single structure integrating deep and surface information, the lines linking nodes in some cases to more than one higher node (each representing a separate 'mother') and in other cases to one or more other nodes on the same level (its 'sisters'), and the features (and in some cases functions) occurring in bundles on higher as well as lower nodes. The only difference between this diagram and fully fledged daughter-dependency structures is that the latter, inevitably, have far more features attached to each of their nodes (as can be seen from the diagrams in later chapters).

To justify generating structures of this type, rather than phrase-markers, is the aim of the whole book; but even at this stage we can bring in the rather negative fact that, so far as I know, there is no direct psycholinguistic evidence that phrase-markers are psychologically real. Moreover, there is some weak evidence in favor of structures like these in that they seem much closer to the traditional notions of sentence structure, centering around a rather minimal amount of constituency (clauses and phrases); a fairly liberal use of the term *belong,* corresponding both to daughter-mother relations (*what belongs* to both clauses at the same time, and so on) and to sister-sister relations (*what* belongs to *happened,* and *you* to *think,* as their respective subjects); and cross-classification of larger units as well as smaller ones (involving terms like 'question' and 'relative clause'). This similarity to traditional grammar lends not only academic respectability but also psychological support, since schoolchildren and their teachers, and other theoretically naïve people, must have found this way of viewing sentence structure reasonably convincing for two thousand years. For all its claims to represent the views of the rationalist philosophers of the Enlightenment, transformational grammar can scarcely trace the notion of the phrase-marker back much further than the neo-Bloomfieldians, the inventors of 'immediate constituent analysis'.

1.2.4. *How a Daughter-dependency Grammar Generates*

For simplicity, we can pretend that all the rules in a daughter-dependency grammar define operations to be executed, one after the other, in order to construct a well-formed structure—though, as we saw in 1.2.2, it may be better to think of them as conditions on well-formedness of ready-made structures. Speaking 'dynamically', then, we can see the process of generating a structure as a series of cycles, one for each constituent, starting from the top of the structure.

First, we apply the *classification rules* (alias 'systems', in 'systemic' grammar) to the simple input 'item' (corresponding to the initial Σ of transformational grammar), to add to it a set of syntactic features (all binary). Classification rules are exactly equivalent to the subcategorization rules of *Aspects of the Theory of Syntax*, except that they are allowed to apply to nodes at any height in the tree. They simply define the combinations of features that are allowed to appear on a single node—for example, they would allow any value (+ or −) of [interrogative] to combine with any value of [main], but would require both to occur with [+ sentence] and prevent them from occurring with [− sentence]. Unlike features in transformational grammars, however, ours are highly constrained by the principles that they should never occur in disjunctive sets—in other words, that they should be maximally 'natural', in the same sense that phonological features have to be natural (see 2.2). This prevents them from suffering from the arbitrariness and ad hocness that so often characterize features in transformational grammars.

Incidentally, it may be worth pointing out that in principle all syntactic features are syntactically justified—and in particular, that they all reflect some *distributional* distinguishing characteristic of the items that share them. For instance, [main] is obviously relevant to distribution: it distinguishes clauses that can stand alone [+ main] from those that can't [− main]; and similarly for [interrogative], though here the distributional difference is found only in embedded clauses ([+ interrogative] clauses can occur with verbs like *ask,* but not with those like *think*), and is then applied to main clauses as well in order to simplify the grammar. No features, in other words, are relevant *just* to semantics—for instance, if the difference between 'positive' and 'negative' were found to be irrelevant to the syntactic distribution of clauses, it wouldn't be reflected by a feature of the clause, [± negative]. This principle of keeping syntactic features syntactic is more consistent with the 'autonomous' view of syntax discussed in 1.2.1 than earlier versions of systemic grammar have been.

Having built up a bundle of features for the top node, we must take the next step—start building up features for its daughters.

(The bundles of features normally aren't complete until the classification rules have reapplied to the daughters in the cyclic fashion explained below.) There are a number of different types of rule for doing this: some add new features by rules that are sensitive to the features already present, and others define the order in which the daughters bearing these features must appear in the structure. The details can be left till the next chapter, and in this section we can simply lump all the rule-types together, with the name 'structure-building rules'.

After the structure-building rules have applied, the cycle starts all over again, this time taking the features on one of the daughters as input. Since every daughter must have some of its features already specified (otherwise, by definition, it wouldn't have been introduced yet and therefore couldn't be a daughter), some of the classification rules have no work to do, except for checking that any features that have already been combined, by the structure-building rules, are allowed to combine. In most cases, though, there are some classification rules that do represent free selections, between + and −; for instance, the verb will have been specified as either finite or nonfinite, but if it is finite, there is still a free choice between making it [+ past] and [− past].

The cycle continues, with structure-building rules alternating with classification rules, until there are no more rules left to apply. At this point, the syntactic structure in the strict sense of the word is complete. However, to produce the equivalent of a transformational syntactic structure, it still remains to insert particular lexical items, to distinguish, for instance, between 'He ate an apple' and 'He ate a pear'. As I explained in 1.2.1 above, there is no *syntactic* difference between these two sentences—the only difference is in their meanings and pronunciations, in the obvious sense. Accordingly, 'lexical insertion' takes the form of a search for items in the lexicon that have syntactic features compatible with those attached to the terminal nodes of the syntactic structure; when suitable items are found, their phonological contents can be added to the phonological structure, and their semantic contents to the semantic structure.

The cycle can be best represented as in fig. 7.

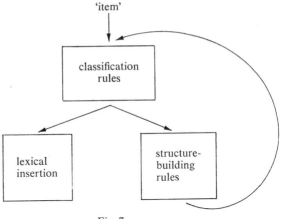

Fig. 7

If you want to generate an arbitrary 'item', select an arbitrary combination of features which the classification rules allow to combine with each other, then apply the structure-building rules to these features, generating partial sets of features for the daughters, then consult the classification rules again for each of the daughters, and so on, until all you can do is to relate the syntactic structure to structures on other levels, via (among other things) the lexical-insertion rules.

The explanation could have been given in 'static' terms instead of dynamic ones. If you have a sentence structure and you want to check that it's well-formed, first make sure that all the feature-combinations attached to all the nodes are combinations that are permitted—if there is a combination that isn't allowed explicitly by the classification rules, then the structure must be ill-formed. Then you check that the relations among the different nodes are permitted by the structure-building rules, which can be seen as constraints that are imposed on the features of one node by those of its mother and of its sisters. If this test is passed as well, the syntactic structure as such must be well-formed.

Seen in these terms, of course, the notion of a 'cycle' is meaningless—it makes no difference whereabouts in the tree you start looking for defects, as they will show up as defects from whichever angle you approach them. This is completely true of daughter-dependency trees, since, as we shall see in the next chapter, all constraints are *local,* involving relations among features that are either on the same node, or on nodes related as sisters or as daughter and mother.

1.3. Some Attractions of Daughter-dependency Grammar

There are empirical arguments in favor of daughter-dependency grammar, which we shall be considering in later chapters. At this stage, however, there are already a few general virtues of the theory that are worth pointing out. To some extent, it is a matter of taste whether you see these characteristics as virtues at all, so I wouldn't claim too much for them as evidence for the superiority of daughter-dependency grammar over transformational grammar.

The most noticeable characteristic of daughter-dependency syntax, compared with transformational syntax, is probably its *concreteness:* in particular, there are no 'underlying' elements that get deleted in the course of the derivation, nor are there any underlying orders of elements that get changed into other orders. There are a number of reasons why you might consider this a virtue. First, it rules out the kind of highly abstract syntactic structure typical of generative semantics, by simply not providing the apparatus for relating such structures to surface patterns —in contrast with the 'interpretive semantics' approach of Chomsky and, for instance, Jackendoff (1972), where the apparatus of transformations is there, and has to be specially constrained if very abstract deep structures are to be ruled out. Of course, if you think abstraction in syntactic structures is a good thing, then you won't be impressed by this property of daughter-dependency grammar. And second, the concreteness of daughter-dependency syntax makes the boundary between syntax and semantics completely clear: as soon as you need to postulate elements or orders of elements different from those in the surface string, you must, by definition, be in semantics. Again, linguists who don't believe there is a boundary between semantics and syntax won't be impressed.

Almost as important is the fact that daughter-dependency syn-

tax generates a *single, integrated structure* for each sentence—
that is, a structure which integrates relatively deep and relatively
surface facts into a single whole, in the way we have outlined.
This has a number of advantages over transformational grammar
with its *series* of structures for each sentence. For one thing, it
means that *all* the rules relating semantic and syntactic structures
to one another refer to the *same* syntactic structure—in contrast
with Chomsky's 'extended standard theory' (1970), in which
some semantic interpretation rules refer to deep structure and
others to surface structure, and the outputs of the two sets of
rules have to be then mapped onto one another in some as yet
unexplained way (by another set of rules?). As Chomsky has
shown, some semantic rules need to refer to a structure that
shows, for instance, whether a noun-phrase is direct object or
'underlying' subject, and others need to refer to one which shows,
for instance, whether a noun-phrase containing *many* is before or
after *not;* in a transformational grammar these are different structures, in a daughter-dependency grammar they are the same.

Another reason why it is helpful to have an integrated syntactic structure is that there are rules relating syntax to phonology
that need to have access to both 'deep' and 'surface' information.
For instance, to the extent that appositive and defining relative
clauses have different intonation patterns, the distinction must be
made by a rule that is sensitive to the difference between them—
which in most transformational analyses has been lost by the
time surface structure is reached, but would be shown in the single syntactic structure of daughter-dependency syntax. Daughter-
dependency syntax has similar advantages over transformational
grammar in handling reduced forms of verbs, which have been
shown to require 'global' rules in transformational grammar
(Lakoff 1970a), but which can apparently be handled quite easily in daughter-dependency grammar, using a rule that applies
only if the verb has a link to a sister on its right (as in 'She's in
a good mood' but not in *'She's in a couple of days time', with
the complement understood).

A third advantage of the integrated syntactic structure is that
it simplifies the task of lexical insertion: in transformational
grammar, the lexicon needs to be consulted at two completely

separate stages of the derivation, once just after the phrase-structure rules have been applied, to insert ordinary lexical items, and once after the transformations have applied, to insert items that either weren't represented in the deep structure (such as the *do* and *there* that get inserted by transformation), or couldn't reasonably be given a phonological form until transformations like (surface) case-assignment has applied (as with *I* versus *me*) (see Stockwell, Schachter and Partee 1973, Hudson 1976*a*). In a daughter-dependency grammar, on the other hand, there is no need to specify any lexical items at all until the whole syntactic structure is fully generated, and then, of course, the lexicon can specify all morphemes at once (by introducing their phonological structures and, where relevant, their meanings). This approach has the added advantage of not introducing semantic and phonological features into the syntactic structure, as transformational grammar does, although neither type of information ever needs to be referred to (I believe) in the syntax itself (see again Hudson 1976*a*).

Apart from the strictly linguistic advantages of integrated syntactic structures, they also seem to have a priori advantages over transformational structures from a psychological point of view, in that it is clear what structures purport to have psychological reality and which don't: the only syntactic structures which should be psychologically real are complete ones—i.e. just one per sentence. In transformational grammar, there has been a great deal of confusion over the status of structures other than the deep structure and the surface structure (see Chomsky 1972: 66, 70 for two conflicting views on their status, within the same article!). But even if it's claimed that only deep and surface structures should have psychological validity, there are big problems, since the only aspects of deep structure that can confidently be expected to have psychological validity are those which distinguish subjects and objects and so on, and which define dependency relations among elements—but this is the kind of information that a daughter-dependency structure gives along with the more surface information. In contrast with these aspects of deep structure, other respects in which deep structures differ from surface structures seem much less likely to be psychologically valid.

For instance, it seems unlikely that anyone will ever be able to prove experimentally that there is an underlying order of elements different from the surface order that has psychological reality; and it seems highly unlikely that this *could* be shown, considering how small a part appeals to intuition ever play in arguments in favor of such underlying orders. Would one, for example, really expect to find psychological evidence for the reality of the underlying order 'He—past—have—*en*—be—*ing*—swim' for 'He had been swimming'? Evidence for a special link between the *have* and the *-en,* perhaps, but surely not evidence for an underlying structure in which they were *next* to one another?

A rather similar advantage of daughter-dependency grammar is the relative ease with which a structure can be assigned mechanically (i.e. by computer) to a sentence: there is no need to reconstruct a whole chain of structures, starting with the surface structure and going back step by step until deep structure is reached, before the syntactic structure can be related to a semantic interpretation. Instead, it is possible to build up the syntactic structure, bit by bit, at the same time as the semantic interpretation (though the two structures are in principle different). This has been recognized as a major attraction of 'systemic grammar' in general by workers in the field of artificial intelligence, since Winograd (1972; see for example Davey 1974). To the extent that successes in artificial intelligence have a bearing on the structure of the human mind, the results so far seem to support the view of syntax as a set of rules that generate a *single* syntactic structure rather than a whole chain of them for each sentence.

The relatively concrete and integrated syntactic structures generated by a daughter-dependency grammar might have attractions for other potential users of syntactic analyses, such as language teachers or students of sociologically conditioned variation or of literary uses of language. I should be happy if this were so, but the case for such structures in the rest of this book will rest entirely on their strictly linguistic advantages: that grammars that generate them are better, as representations of the realities of language structure, than transformational grammars are.

2 Classification Rules

2.1. Introduction

Classification rules, as their name implies, have the task of classifying syntactic items, in the sense that they define the set of classificatory pigeonholes in terms of which items are classified. The pigeonholes are defined by bundles of features, so the role of the classification rules is to say which features combine with which in bundles attached to single nodes. They have nothing to say about the relations between features on different nodes—in other words, about syntagmatic relations; not surprisingly, then, the formal properties of classification rules are extremely simple, and the notation used can be simple. As readers familiar with transformational grammar will see, the formal properties of classification rules are exactly the same as those of Chomsky's context-free 'subcategorization rules' (1965: 82), although the role they play in the grammar is somewhat different, as we shall see later. Like subcategorization rules, classification rules relate two sets of features to each other: one set is treated as 'input', the other as 'output', and the latter is seen as depending on the former. For example, Chomsky's rule (ibid.)

$$[+ \text{ common}] \rightarrow [\pm \text{ count}]$$

can be translated into prose like this: the features [+ count] and [– count] are permitted in the same bundle as the feature [+ common], and wherever the latter occurs, one or the other of the former must occur; or, more simply, any item which is [+ common] must be either [+ count] or [– count], and this distinction is irrelevant to items that don't have the feature [+ common] (unless, of course, some other rule explicitly allows them to occur with some other feature).

The notation used for classification rules is slightly different from the transformational notation, since we shall be using the arrow exclusively to show syntagmatic relations, as we shall see in the next chapter. Instead of arrows, we shall use semicolons. If we were to include the equivalent of Chomsky's rule into a daughter-dependency grammar, it would look like this:

+ common: ± count.

Its effect would be just the same as that of Chomsky's rule: to generate bundles of features containing either [+ common, + count] or [+ common, – count], and to rule out any bundle that contained [+ common] without either [+ count] or [– count].

As with Chomsky's rule, both the left-hand side of the rule and the right-hand side can be internally complex, in that either may contain a *conjunction* (but not a disjunction) of features. To take an actual rule from our grammar in Appendix 1 as an example, the right-hand side can contain quite a large number of features which by definition define contrasts which cut across each other:

C.27, 31, 32 + verb: ± auxiliary, ± finite, ± transitive.

(The question of whether this represents just one rule, as I have been implying so far, or three separate rules, as the numbering implies, seems to be just a matter of notation: if this notation is used, it can be shown as one rule, whereas if the network notation which we shall introduce below is used, it comes out as three separate rules.) This rule defines eight different classes of verb, all of which have members (see the lexicon in section D of Appendix 1).

Just as the right-hand side of a classification rule can be a conjunction of features, so can the left-hand side, the only difference being that in the former instance the values of the features are all unspecified, while in the latter instance they are specified either as plus or as minus, as the case may be. For example, if forms like *isn't, can't* and *don't* are treated as single words (i.e. as single, syntagmatically indivisible syntactic elements), they must be distinguished from the corresponding forms without -*n't,* so we need a feature [± neg-Aux] (rule C.35), with plus for the former and minus for the latter. But this contrast applies only to verbs that are both finite (cf. **beingn't*) and also auxiliaries (cf. **comesn't*), so we can restrict it to the combination of features [+ finite, + Aux]:

C.35 + finite, + Aux: ± neg-Aux

Had we had a single feature on the left-hand side of the rule, feature-combinations would have been generated that would need to be ruled out somewhere else in the grammar—for example, if the left-hand side had been just [+ finite], the classification rules on their own would allow combinations including [+ neg-Aux, – auxiliary], but since there are no verbs other than auxiliaries that contain *-n't,* some other way would have to be found to rule this combination out. With the conjunction of features on the left-hand side, however, this is unnecessary.

I have already said that classification rules are formally identical to Chomsky's context-sensitive subcategorization rules, but there is another comparison to be made, with the 'systems' of other versions of systemic grammar, including the one represented in Hudson (1971). Broadly speaking, classification rules are the same as systems in their form (I shall return to the only formal differences shortly), and they have precisely the same function in the grammar (unlike subcategorization rules); the most obvious differences are simply in notation. Systems have an arrow (which has lost its head by Hudson 1974) between the two sides of the rule, and the right-hand side is written two-dimensionally; for instance, Chomsky's rule would look like this when written as a system:

$$+ \text{common} \longrightarrow \begin{bmatrix} + \text{count} \\ - \text{count} \end{bmatrix}$$

A set of interrelated systems can be laid out graphically as a 'system-network', by treating the right-hand side of one rule as the left-hand side of another rule; and a convention for using brackets (square and curly) allows one to represent systems with a *set* of features on the left or right. The two classification rules quoted above would be represented as in fig. 8 if we translated them into a system-network.

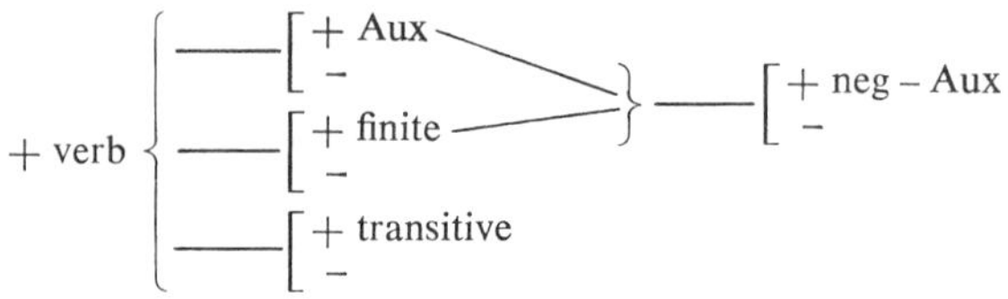

Fig. 8

This type of presentation has many attractions and advantages, but I haven't used it at all in the body of this book for two reasons: it makes daughter-dependency grammar look more different from transformational grammar with respect to this type of grammar than it really is; and it seems possible, I find, for transformational linguists to misinterpret system-networks as representations of sentence structure (improbable though this may seem). However, for the sake of linguists who find networks helpful, I have given all the classification rules in Appendix 1 in both notations.

Apart from these rather trivial matters of notation, there are two formal differences between classification rules and systems. First, the features in classification rules are all binary, whereas in systems there may be more than two features on the right-hand side, as mutually exclusive alternatives (see McCord 1975, who also favors binary features in systemic grammar). I have never found any convincing examples of contrasts that have to be treated as involving three or more alternatives in syntax, so I have made the assumption that such contrasts are in principle impossible, and adopted Chomsky's plus/minus notation. The onus seems to be on supporters of nonbinary contrasts to prove that such contrasts exist, and can't be reanalyzed in terms of binary contrasts. On the other hand, I have to admit that the plus/minus notation can be a nuisance when there is no good reason for treating one of the alternatives rather than the other as the 'marked', or abnormal, one of the pair—for instance, if one were to classify relative clauses as 'reduced' or 'nonreduced', should one talk of [± reduced] or [± full]? At present I have nothing useful to say on this matter.

The other difference between classification rules and systems is that the left-hand side of the latter may consist of, or contain, a *dis*junction of features: some particular contrast can apply to items that have *either* of two (or more) features. This facility makes a grammar much more powerful than it would be if sets of features had to be conjunctions, since sets no longer need to define 'natural' classes, in the sense of Halle (1964): a class defined by means of a smaller number of features than any sub-class within it. We shall return to this question in the next section, so I need say no more here than that I haven't found any convincing examples of contrasts applying to disjunctions of features, and once again the onus is on advocates of the more powerful type of grammar to show that the extra power is in fact needed.

The reason for preferring the term 'classification rule' to 'system' or 'subcategorization rule' is that it is much more self-explanatory than the former to linguists not brought up in the British tradition, and somewhat less cumbersome than the latter —which, moreover, is used in the transformational literature to refer to rules that take account of the syntagmatic environment.

2.2. Constraints on Classification by Features

One of the main dangers facing any grammar which makes use of features, as daughter-dependency grammar does, is that they may become too powerful—and the grammarian's life may become too easy, because of this. Since features can, in principle, combine freely with one another, it would be possible to write a grammar in which there is a separate feature corresponding to each place in each construction, so that each such place would in effect define its own distributional class. There would then be no reason to be surprised if each of the various distributional classes had a more or less different set of items as its members —whereas in fact there seems to be a marked tendency for different environments to define either the same or similar classes, and, moreover, for items that occur in similar environments to have similar internal structures. Admittedly, it is likely that a grammar would be extremely complicated if each different envi-

ronment defined a different feature, whereas one that maximized
the use of features (by allowing different environments to be
associated with the same feature) would be less complicated,
taken overall. However, it would be interesting to know if there
are any restrictions which can be imposed in general on the use
of features, so that grammars of the first kind (among others)
would be ruled out in principle, rather than simply by applying
an evaluation metric such as simplicity. In other words, it would
be good to know if there are any kinds of properties, with respect
to the use of features, that are never found in grammars that
score well for simplicity, or whatever the best evaluation metric
should be. On the basis of my very limited experience of writing
grammars for English, I should like to propose a candidate for
constraints on features: that the classes defined by them are *natural,* in the sense of Halle (1964).

We discussed this constraint briefly in the previous section, in
connection with the formal properties of classification rules. I
said there that the left-hand side of a classification rule never
contains a *dis*junction of features, although it can contain a conjunction of them. In this section, though, we have to generalize
the principle to cover other types of rule, including many of the
types that we shall be considering in the next chapter. For most
types of rule, it seems that they never involve disjunctions of
features—indeed, there is only one kind of rule that consistently
involves disjunctions, namely function-assignment rules (see 3.5
and Appendix 1, section J). This is a strong claim, and may well
not be true; but the fact that at least a large part of the grammar
of English can be covered by a grammar without disjunctions
suggests that this may turn out to be a general property of syntax.
If it does, it will go a long way toward explaining why syntax is
so stable, since it inevitably makes the different parts of the grammar much more interdependent than they would be if disjunctions were permitted. For instance, a new class of items couldn't
suddenly be permitted in an environment unless it had enough
features in common with the class already permitted there for
the two classes to be referred to together by a single set of features with no disjunctions; and this means that the change in

distribution has to be compatible with the classification rules, or that the classification rules have to change to keep step with the distributional change. Since the classification rules themselves are subject to the same ban on disjunctions, it isn't likely to be easy to find a new set of classification rules which both allow the distributional change and also satisfy the disjunction ban—so change itself is unlikely.

There is one particularly interesting place in a grammar for English where it appears that a disjunction *is* needed, and which has considerable theoretical interest for other reasons, so it may not be out of place to say a word on it here. The question is, at first sight, a rather trivial one, which most linguists would be happy to leave to their students to solve while they concerned themselves with more important and difficult things (but see Morgan 1972 and Vanek 1970*b*): how does one establish concord between subjects and verbs in English (and, I assume, in many other languages too). The problem is that the distinctions between different types of subject to which the rule must refer seem initially to be quite chaotic. For instance, if the subject consists of a conjunction of noun-phrases, it takes 'plural' concord in the verb, but if it consists of a disjunction of noun-phrases which are themselves singular, it takes singular concord:

The boy and the girl have/*has just come in.
The boy or the girl *have/has just come in.

Moreover, noun-phrases count as plural for this rule not only if they have a plural noun as head, but also if they have a collective noun such as *committee* or *crowd,* provided this is taken to refer semantically to the members of the collectivity as separate individuals; and, worse still, measure nouns like *heap* and *bagful* count as singular or plural according to the number of an embedded *of*-phrase:

Only a little heap of bones/*dust were left.

If the different kinds of subject are to be distinguished on the level of syntax, there is no doubt that the concord rule would need to refer to a disjunction of features, since there is no other syntactic reason for aligning, say, *a little heap of bones* with noun-phrases containing plural head nouns in contrast with *a little heap of dust*. Not only does this conclusion contradict what we have found in studying other cases, about disjunctions being unnecessary; but, like any disjunction, this one makes the set of items to which the rule refers seem completely arbitrary, since it amounts to an admission that there is no unifying principle behind the grouping. In fact, of course, the groupings to which the subject-verb concord rule refers are anything but arbitrary, since wherever a noun-phrase with a singular noun as head takes a plural verb it refers to a group of individuals, as individuals, rather than to a single entity—and vice versa. On the other hand, it won't do to simply say that the rule refers to *semantic* properties of the subject, since nouns like *oats* and *scales* (as in *bathroom scales*) take a plural form of the verb although they are semantically singular. The correct generalization seems to be this:

> Plural forms of verbs are used if the subject is *either* syntactically *or* semantically plural; otherwise singular forms of the verb are used.

(This generalization applies only to third-person subjects, and would need slight modification to make it apply to other persons.)

An analysis reflecting this generalization would clearly be more insightful than one formulated in terms of purely syntactic properties of the subject, but it faces two large problems: first, it still involves a disjunction (either semantic or syntactic plurality), and second, it refers to two different levels of analysis, unlike any of the standard syntactic rules. (Notice incidentally that it doesn't help to abandon the distinction between syntax and semantics, as in generative semantics, since there would then be no way of stating the distinction between syntactic and semantic plurality, there being only *one* kind of plurality.) However, precisely because there are so many problems in the way of formulating a syntactic rule for subject-verb concord, one is encouraged to think it might not be a syntactic rule at all. The alternative which strikes me as the most attractive is to treat it as a *morphological* rule: some of the rules relating verb-features to phonological shapes will be context-sensitive, and able to take account of the syntactic and semantic properties of the verb's subject (which, incidentally, is very easy to identify in a daughter-dependency syntactic structure, since it is labeled SUBJECT, and connected to the verb by a sister-dependency trace line; compare the structures given as examples in chapters 3 and 4). One advantage of treating the subject-verb concord rule as a morphological rule would be that different verbs could be sensitive to different features of the subject, and in particular the verb *be* could be treated differently from all other verbs (it makes a singular/plural distinction in the past tense, and a distinction between first-person singular and other persons in the present tense, unlike any other verb). If, on the other hand, the rule is treated as a syntactic rule, there are two alternatives, both more or less unacceptable: *be* can be identified syntactically, so that a different rule can apply to *be* compared with the rule for other verbs (and similarly, of course, for modal verbs); or the same rule can apply irrespective of the verb, making the maximal number of distinctions for them all. We shall see in chapter 4 that there is no reason to think that all uses of *be* are unified syntactically (see 4.6), so the first of the alternatives disappears; and the second alternative is clumsy, at best. In any case, as we have just seen, there are other problems if subject-verb concord is treated as a syntactic rule, so it seems best to assume that it will be a morphological rule, or set of rules, instead. It may be that the same is true of all concord rules, in fact, but this is not the place to extend the discussion further.

The point of this discussion of subject-verb concord in English has been mainly to show how counter-examples to the 'no disjunctions' principle can be disposed of, by taking one of the most promising candidates as an example. However, the example is a fortunate one, since it has allowed me to say something about the treatment of morphological concord rules at the same time. I shall have nothing more to say about such rules in the rest of this book.

In conclusion, I should explain that it is very much easier to write grammars that do contain disjunctions of features than grammars that don't, and that all I have claimed here is that it is *possible* to write the latter kind of grammar, and that there are no reasons for thinking that disjunctions improve a grammar—by making it in other respects much simpler, for instance. It would be disingenuous to claim that I arrived at my grammar without paying any attention to the use of disjunctions; on the contrary, for some time now I have been suspicious of them, so I set myself the goal of avoiding them as far as possible. The result is a grammar which classifies items quite differently in some respects from any transformational grammar that I know of, or, for that matter, from any other kind of grammar. For instance, the first classification rule (or set of rules) classifies every syntactic item as a sentence or a nonsentence and *also* as a phrase or a nonphrase and as a nominal or a nonnominal:

C.1, 2, 3 'item': ± sentence, ± phrase, ± nominal

One of the benefits of this analysis is that it helps in the elimination of disjunctions, but it has other advantages too, such as that it allows a more natural analysis of embedded sentences than the transformational analyses do, as I shall explain in the next section. It seems reasonable to assume, in the light of analyses such as this, that imposing the naturalness constraint, with its corollary that no disjunctions should be allowed, at worst doesn't stop us writing grammars that work, and probably leads to improvements in grammars.

2.3. Classification of Sentences and Phrases

The examples of classification rules given in 2.1 involved features of the verb—i.e. of a particular class of word. They were deliberately chosen to avoid controversy (many transformational linguists would probably accept syntactic features on verbs), since the aim was simply to introduce the notation and formal properties for classification rules. In this section we turn to more controversial matters: the assignment of features to higher nodes. As we have seen, it would be impossible to integrate such features into a transformational grammar, without abandoning the notion of phrase-structure rules (and, consequently, of transformational grammar as a whole). What I have to show, then, is why it is *desirable* to have features on higher nodes. The following arguments can be added to those already given by transformationalists, notably Chomsky (1970), Vanek (1970*a* and *b*) and Schachter (1972). (Schachter argues that, say, extraposed relative clauses need to be distinguished from extraposed complement-clauses in shallow structure, to stop them from being coordinated with each other; this seems to imply the need for features on higher nodes.)

Let us take as an example the features introduced by the rule C.1–3 just quoted. This rule can be thought of as an abbreviation of three rules:

C.1 'item': ± sentence
C.2 'item': ± phrase
C.3 'item': ± nominal

One advantage of this analysis is that it allows one to classify an item as being *both* a clause [+ sentence] *and* as a noun-phrase [+ phrase, + nominal], without giving priority to one feature over the other. (The extensions of the eight classes defined by the three features can be seen from the paradigm in section A of Appendix 1.) It is easy to show that this is precisely what is wanted for clauses whose verb is a gerund—in transformational terms, for clauses containing the complementizer POSS-ING, such as the italicized clauses in the following (Chomsky's 'gerundive nominals'—1970: 187):

Climbing mountains is hard work.
John/John's coming late was a nuisance.
He enjoyed *watching the girl*.
He came in without/after *ringing the bell*.

On the one hand, such clauses (which I shall refer to, for short, as 'gerund-clauses') need to be classified as clauses (or sentences —I shall use the two terms interchangeably), for all the reasons given, for instance, by Chomsky (ibid.): they can be negated, they allow bare noun-phrases rather than prepositional phrases as object, they allow auxiliary verbs and so on. But at the same time, they need to be classified in the same way as ordinary noun-phrases, since their distribution is just the same: they can occur as subjects, objects and objects of prepositions, and they can't be extraposed except in contexts where noun-phrases too can be extraposed:

> To write the book/writing the book/the job took two years.
> It took two years to write the book/*writing the book/
> *the job.
> To see them together/seeing them together/the way he looks at her is nice.
> It's nice to see them together/seeing them together/
> the way he looks at her.

This relation is precisely the one reflected by our classification: gerund-clauses (and no others) are characterized by the features [+ sentence, + phrase, + nominal], so that they participate not only in all the rules for sentences but also in those for noun-phrases, which are defined by the features [+ phrase, + nominal]. The analysis even explains why the subject of a gerund-clause can be a possessive (*John's, his*): it is a direct daughter of a node with the features [+ phrase, + nom], just like a possessive inside an ordinary noun-phrase. Provided there is some way of identifying the subject position with the position of the possessive in an ordinary noun-phrase (maybe simply as the initial noun-phrase, since gerund-clauses don't allow any other noun-phrase to precede the subject), it should be possible to formulate a single rule to cover both cases, to the effect that an (initial) noun-phrase immediately dominated by [+ phrase, + nom] should be possessive.

Consider now the standard transformational treatment of gerund-clauses. The intention is precisely to show all the relations that we discussed in the last paragraph, but the properties of transformational grammar make it impossible to do so. It is easy to show one or the other of the two alignments (to clauses and to noun-phrases), but one can't show *both* of them, precisely because only one class label (S or NP) can be attached to any one node (except at the bottom of the tree, of course, which doesn't concern us here). Accordingly, if the aim is to classify gerund-clauses both as clauses and as noun-phrases, we need to have two nodes corresponding to the same item, one for each class name. In the standard analysis this is achieved by treating it as a noun-phrase with a clause as its only constituent:

NP

S

(The alternative, with S dominating NP, isn't worth considering, since it has no advantages over the standard analysis, and all its disadvantages.) This analysis has two crucial shortcomings: it can't be justified on independent grounds, and it doesn't in fact achieve what it is meant to achieve.

First, the lack of independent support for this analysis of gerund-clauses as constituents of noun-phrases. There are two arguments that are used to support a similar analysis for complement-clauses introduced by *that* (or zero) and by *(for) . . . to . . . ,* but neither of them works for gerund-clauses. The first argument is that such clauses can occur in apposition to an overt noun and determiner, as in 'the fact that . . . ' and 'the desire to . . . ', where it is quite natural to treat the clause as a constituent of a noun-phrase; if one accepts deletion rules in general, it isn't too hard to accept that a rule can delete a head noun and determiner such as *the fact,* leaving the originally appositive clause as the only surviving constituent of the noun-phrase. This argument fails to apply to gerund-clauses, since they don't occur at all in this kind of appositive relation to a determiner and noun (cf. the *fact/ *desire/*enjoyment/*need leaving). The second argument involves the *it* which appears as subject if the complement-clause is extraposed, as in 'It is clear that . . . '. If complement-clauses are treated as the leftovers of a noun-phrase, then this *it* can be treated as another part of the same deep-structure noun-phrase. There are problems with this analysis even for clauses other than gerund-clauses—for instance, is there really no connection between this *it* and the one found in cleft sentences ('It was John who . . . ') and the one found with weather verbs and adjectives

('It rained')? But in any case the argument can't be extended to gerund-clauses, since they don't allow extraposition except in contexts where ordinary noun-phrases can be extraposed, as I pointed out above; and presumably there is no way in which the standard analysis could be extended to cover the *it* in sentences where the extraposed item is a noun-phrase, such as *the funny way he moves his mouth* in 'It amuses me the funny way he moves his mouth'. Once again, the argument used for analyzing other kinds of complement-clauses as constituents of noun-phrases turns out not to apply to gerund-clauses, and until further arguments for this analysis can be found which *are* relevant to gerund-clauses, we can conclude that it has no independent justification, other than the need to show that gerund-clauses are noun-phrases as well as sentences.

We now turn to the question of whether the standard analysis really *does* show the similarities between gerund-clauses and other, ordinary, noun-phrases. There are two kinds of similarity to be shown: similarity (indeed, identity) of distribution, and similarity of internal structure with respect to the possessive noun-phrase acting as subject or determiner, as the case may be. The first similarity is shown, it is true, in that gerund-clauses are automatically permitted wherever noun-phrases can occur, and only there. However, the problem is that the same is true of other kinds of complement-clauses, although their distributions are *not* the same as for noun-phrases—for example, they can't occur as complements of most prepositions, and they can occur with verbs like *seem* which don't allow any ordinary noun-phrases as complements. Moreover, Ross's constraint on 'internal Ss' (1967), to the effect that an embedded sentence must be either at the front or at the end, but not in the middle, of the matrix sentence, does apply to other kinds of embedded sentences, but doesn't apply to gerund-clauses; for instance, only the latter can occur as a subject inverted with the auxiliary of the matrix clause:

Does seeing them together/*that they're together upset you?

How can these distributional differences between gerund-clauses and ordinary noun-phrases, on the one hand, and other types of

embedded clauses, on the other hand, be shown in a transformational grammar? In the standard analysis, they are shown by
means of differences in the rules that insert the various complementizers, and (presumably) by making the internal-S constraint
sensitive to the differences among the complementizers, so that it
applies to THAT and FOR-TO but not to POSS-ING. From the present point of view, this approach has a big drawback: having
shown the identity of gerund-clauses to ordinary noun-phrases
by means of the NP node dominating them, we must show the
identity a *second* time, by saying in which contexts POSS-ING can
occur; and by chance, so it will appear, these contexts are just
the same as those in which ordinary noun-phrases can occur. An
alternative analysis is proposed by Bresnan (1970, 1972)—that
complementizers should be present already in deep structure, so
that the differences among them can be treated as genuine distributional differences, reflecting the co-occurrence restrictions
imposed by verbs on their complements, rather than being the
result of different contexts allowing different complementizers to
be inserted transformationally. For all its attractions, this approach doesn't solve our present problem, since Bresnan excludes gerunds from her analysis altogether, and it's not at all
clear how her analysis could be extended to cover them. In any
case, her analysis of the other complementizers has other problems—for instance, if you generate complementizers as sisters of
S in the base, by phrase-structure rules, there is no way of preventing, say, THAT from occurring with a main clause. It seems,
then, that neither the standard analysis nor Bresnan's alternative in fact shows the distributional similarities between gerund-
clauses and ordinary noun-phrases, in contrast with other types
of embedded clauses.

The other kind of similarity between gerund-clauses and noun-
phrases is in the occurrence of the possessive either as determiner
in an ordinary noun-phrase or as subject in a gerund-clause. As
we saw above, the daughter-dependency analysis treats both possessives as daughters of a node labeled [+ phrase, + nom] (together with other features, of course); and since both possessives
are the first noun-phrases in their respective constructions, it is

easy to bring out the similarity between them in the grammar. When we look at the current transformational analyses, we find that this is not the case. Take, first, what I have been referring to as the 'standard' analysis (as represented, for instance, by Jacobs and Rosenbaum 1968 and Burt 1971). Here, the relation between the subject of a gerund and the noun-phrase node dominating it is like this:

In other words, because of the S node intervening between the two NPs, the possessive is shown as a *grand*daughter of the higher noun-phrase, and is no more similar to the possessive in an ordinary noun-phrase than is the subject of any other kind of embedded clause. Whether any other transformational analysis would be able to solve this problem isn't clear, since it's unclear how possessives in ordinary noun-phrases should be treated; but as long as they are dominated by a node representing the determiner constituent (which seems to be a permanent feature of transformational analyses), even Chomsky's '$\overline{\text{X}}$' notation (1970: 210) won't help, since it would be necessary to identify the determiner node in the ordinary noun-phrase with the sentence node in the gerund-clause—something which would surely be very hard to justify. Once again, then, the transformational analysis fails, and apparently *must* fail, to show the similarity between gerund-clauses and ordinary noun-phrases.

To summarize this section so far, we have seen that one advantage that daughter-dependency grammar has over transformational grammar is that it allows gerund-clauses to be classified *both* as clauses *and* as noun-phrases, whereas the best a transformational grammar can do is to treat them as clauses that are *part* of a noun-phrase, albeit the only part. This isn't good enough, since on the one hand the only justification for the analysis is the need to show similarities of distribution and structure between gerund-clauses and ordinary noun-phrases, and on the other hand it doesn't in fact achieve this: all it does is to treat gerund-clauses as constituents of noun-phrases, just like the other types of embedded noun-clause. This illustrates a much more general advantage of daughter-dependency grammar: that it allows internally complex items (such as clauses and phrases) to be *cross-classified* —in this case, with reference to the contrasts between sentence and nonsentence and the contrast between noun-phrases and other items. This is possible because classes such as 'sentence' and 'noun-phrase' are represented by features—rather than by category labels, as in transformational grammar.

Having features on higher nodes produces a number of other advantages for daughter-dependency grammar. We shall now consider two of them: that with such features it is unnecessary to define classes in terms of internal structural markers, and that it is unnecessary to define classes in terms of external syntagmatic environments. In both cases, features allow us to *subclassify* a larger class—say, the class of clauses—in order to reflect some difference.

The use of internal structural markers in order to define classes is very common in transformational grammar. The 'basic' classes are defined by means of labels attached to the node belonging to the item being classified—S, NP, VP and so on—but further subdivisions within this class are defined in terms of elements occurring within the structure of the items concerned (or in terms of the environment, to which we shall turn later). For example, a distinction is needed between two subclasses of clause, interrogative and noninterrogative clauses, and this is made by referring to the presence or absence of the element Q; in other words, any rules that need to single out interrogative clauses in contrast with other types of clause (such as the rules for forming questions, or the strict subcategorization rules for verbs like *ask*) do so by referring to them as 'clauses containing Q'; and similarly if a rule applies to definite noun-phrases but not to indefinite ones, or vice versa, it will need to refer to the definiteness of the determiner inside the noun-phrase. In contrast, both of these distinctions would be made in a daughter-dependency grammar in terms of features of the clause or phrase itself, without specifying how those features are reflected in the item's internal structure—the rules concerned would be able to refer to [+ interrogative] clauses and [+ definite] or [– definite] noun-phrases.

The transformational approach has a number of disadvantages. First, it is inconsistent to refer to some classes in terms of labels on the relevant node and to others in terms of labels on nodes that are dominated by the relevant node. Second, it becomes necessary to allow strict subcategorization rules for verbs to refer to 'nieces' as well as to sisters (as was the original intention in Chomsky 1965: 96), since they need to be able to refer to complementizers and/or 'pre-sentences' (Q, Imp, etc.) *within* the complement-sentence (this is as true of Bresnan's reanalysis, with complementizers dominated by $\overline{S}$, as it is in the standard analysis); this gives strict subcategorization rules much more flexibility than they ought to have, and raises the question of why verbs shouldn't be strictly subcategorized, for instance, with reference to the presence or absence of an object in the complement-sentence, which so far as I know is never relevant in fact. In the daughter-dependency approach, of course, this is not so: the rules equivalent to strict subcategorization rules (sister-dependency rules—see 3.4) can be restricted (as their name suggests) to referring to sisters of the verb, since they can refer to the feature [+ interrogative], for instance, which is a feature of the *whole* complement-clause with a verb like *ask*.

A third disadvantage of the transformational approach is that it necessitates postulating abstract underlying elements to which rules can refer even when these elements don't show up in surface structure (this objection is also made by Householder, 1971: 95). For instance, if we want to distinguish between imperative and nonimperative clauses (as we surely do), we look in vain for an *overt* element which is characteristic of imperative clauses but not of any others. Perhaps the nearest one comes to such a marker is that such clauses contain the bare infinitive as first verb, which in transformational terms corresponds to saying that they lack the element *tense* in their deep structure; so one might consider the possibility of simply making *tense* optional in deep structure, and using it as a marker of 'nonimperative'. However, there are other clauses which also lack *tense*—such as gerund-clauses—and which need to be excluded from the class of 'imperative' clauses, and in any case it's awkward to refer to the *absence* of an element in a rule, so transformational grammars usually reverse the direction of 'markedness', and treat *imperatives* as the clauses that contain a marker, which is missing in nonimperatives, rather than the other way round. The marker which they use, Imp, is never pronounced and amounts, in effect, to a completely arbitrary diacritic, used in lieu of a feature on the clause node—[+ optative], in our grammar (rule C.4). It is worth pointing out that it is arbitrary too in its *position*—why posit this element as occurring at the beginning of the clause, rather than at its end or next to tense? Imperative clauses illustrate the problem of referring to a class that is marked by the absence of some element; but there are other types of problem too. For instance, occasionally one finds classes which are marked by the *order* of elements rather than by the presence (or absence) of any particular element. This is notably true of yes-no direct questions and of the type of conditional clause signaled by inversion of subject and auxiliary ('Had I known he was away, I wouldn't have called'). In both these cases, the formal restrictions on transformational grammars make it necessary to postulate some kind of underlying element (which might be Q or a higher verb, such as *ask,* in the case of interrogatives, and presumably might be *if* for the conditionals). These elements in deep structure tell us more about the properties of transformational grammars than about language.

A final advantage of daughter-dependency grammar in this connection is that it improves the possibility of comparing languages by locating differences either in the features or in the markers of the features, whereas transformational grammars in some cases have to confuse the two. For example, both English and Welsh make a distinction between declarative and interrogative clauses, but in Welsh there are overt markers for *both* classes —a range of declarative particles as well as a range of interrogative ones. In a transformational grammar, Welsh would look rather different from English in its deep structures, since it would (presumably) need Dec as well as Q as a possible pre-sentence element (or however the distinction is to be made). In a daughter-dependency grammar, on the other hand, it would have the same feature distinguishing declarative and interrogative—[± interrogative], rule C.6—and the differences would be simply in the structure-building rules; probably Welsh would have an extra daughter-dependency rule, introducing the declarative particles.

In this section so far, we have considered two main types of advantage arising from the use of features on higher nodes, allowing us to cross-classify and subclassify clauses and phrases: it allows classes such as sentence and noun-phrase to overlap (as in gerund-clauses), and it makes it unnecessary to refer in 'external' rules to the internal structure of a clause or phrase. We now come to the last type of advantage: that features on higher nodes allow one to subclassify clauses and phrases without making the distinctions in terms of the environments in which the items concerned occur. All the examples we shall consider will be clauses, so we can simplify the discussion by referring simply to the analysis of clauses: the fact is that clauses are different from one linguistic context to another, and the question is whether these differences should be treated as in some sense 'inherent' to the clauses themselves, or as the result of 'environmental conditioning'. For example, there are 'main clauses' and there are 'relative clauses', each characterized by a different range of internal structures; should we set up two different distributional classes of clause, each with a different range of contexts in which it can occur, or should we do as in transformational grammar, and say that there is a single distributional class (S) and the context can affect the internal structures of members of this single class in various ways, as shown in a grammar by means of transformations sensitive to the context—namely, in this case, by a relative clause transformation? In most general terms, daughter-dependency grammar favors the use of distributional classes (not having the apparatus for reflecting contextual conditioning), while transformational grammar makes use of rules reflecting contextual conditioning, and lacks the apparatus for making distinctions between distributional subclasses. This is an issue which has received surprisingly little discussion, considering that neither approach is self-evidently right; I shall now try to show that in at least some cases a grammar needs to have the apparatus for making distinctions by means of features on higher nodes, rather than by means of context-sensitive rules like a 'relative-clause–formation' rule; I'll leave it to advocates of the transformational approach to find arguments that a grammar also needs to be able to deal in terms of contextual conditioning in syntax (as opposed, say, to morphology and phonology). I don't know of any such arguments, myself.

To clarify the issue, let us start by reviewing the means by which a transformational grammar can relate differences in the range of surface clauses to differences in the contexts in which they occur. There are two ways: either it can add a 'satellite' structure in the base (such as a 'complementizer' node) as a sister to the clause, or it can introduce the appropriate distinctions by means of transformations sensitive to the clause's context. What it can't do, of course, is add features to the S node in the deep structure. So the transformational approach amounts to a rather strong claim about language structure, that all cases of covariation between the internal structure of a clause and its (external) context can be handled in one or the other of these two ways. I believe this claim to be wrong, for the following reasons.

First, the context can be responsible not only for the presence of an extra element (such as a complementizer) which would otherwise be absent but also for the absence of an element which would otherwise be present—where 'otherwise' means 'in the absence of any context', i.e. in main clauses. The most obvious case of this is the absence of the tense element from some kinds of embedded clause, such as gerund-clauses, infinitive clauses with *for* and *to,* and reduced relative clauses. It is easy to show that tense, with its forced choice between past and present, should be absent from these clauses not only in their surface structures but also in their deep structures: the tense needed, for semantic reasons, would have to vary according to the tense of a higher verb, since a past tense may be 'understood' in a past-tense context, but not in a present-tense context (Anita Hochster helped me to improve on an earlier formulation of this rule):

The man sitting next to me (= 'who *was* [or *is*] sitting next to me') stood up.
The man sitting next to me (= 'who *is* sitting next to me') keeps on standing up.

This is true of all these clauses with nonfinite verbs, and it is not true, it should be noted, that the present tense can be used in a 'neutral' way in other kinds of clause (see Hudson 1973 for a slightly fuller discussion). The problem for a transformational grammar is, of course, that there is no way to prevent tense from being inserted into the deep structures of sentences like these, since the rule that inserts tense would have to be sensitive to the context of the whole clause—whereas phrase-structure rules are not allowed to be sensitive to any kind of context, let alone a context as remote as that. If, on the other hand, it were possible to subclassify clauses by means of features on higher nodes, it would be possible to distinguish clauses containing tense (or the equivalent in daughter-dependency grammar, [+ finite]) from those that lack it, by means of clause-features, and then restrict the contexts in which such clauses can occur, by letting the distributional rules (equivalent to transformational grammar's phrase-structure rules) refer to these features rather than simply to the class of clauses as a whole.

It might be thought, incidentally, that a possible solution to this problem within the transformational approach would be to extract tense from the rest of the clause, and treat it as a satellite constituent, with the rest of the clause as a sister. There are two ways in which this might be achieved: either following Bresnan, with tense and the rest of the clause dominated jointly by $\bar{\text{S}}$ (so that tense would have a status like that of a complementizer), or following McCawley (1971), with tense as a 'higher verb' (see fig. 9).

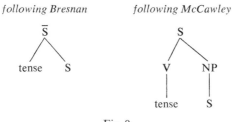

following Bresnan   *following McCawley*

Fig. 9

However, neither of these alternatives does in fact solve the problem, if only because the relation between tense and the context is too indirect for ordinary phrase-structure rules to reflect, and Bresnan's distinction between S and S̄ couldn't be used to reflect simply the presence or absence of tense, since it's also needed to reflect the presence or absence of complementizers, some of which can occur where tense can't occur (notably, FOR-TO).

Another problem for the transformational approach is that it works convincingly only where a given transformation applies in just one context (or in a range of contexts which can easily be collapsed into a single 'structural description'). Because of the way that transformations are formulated, with the relevant context built into the rule as part of the rule, whenever the same operation occurs in two uncollapsible contexts, it must be reflected by two separate rules; and to the extent that the operations concerned are complex, this represents a missed generalization. The missed generalization is even more serious, of course, if more than one operation is involved, since it would then be not one transformation but a series of them which would need to be repeated in the grammar. A relevant example is the use of what I shall call 'participial clauses'—clauses whose first verb is a participle (i.e. an *ing*-form or *en*-form verb—but excluding gerundive uses of *ing*-form verbs). Such clauses occur as alternatives to full relative clauses, as in the examples quoted above to illustrate the absence of tense; and in the standard transformational analysis they are, in fact, derived from full relative clauses by 'whiz-deletion' (deleting the relative pronoun subject and *is*).

The problem is that precisely the same range of clauses can occur with an adverbial function, as in:

Owning a large house, he can do a lot of entertaining.
Walking down the high street I ran into Mrs. Jones.
Defeated at the last general election, he plans to give up
    politics in favor of a business career.

Clearly there is no way in which the two environments could be collapsed into one, so that a single rule could derive both sets of clauses; so if they are indeed derived transformationally from unreduced clauses, then a different transformation will be needed for each context. The standard derivation of reduced relative clauses is unworkable, since there need not be an underlying *is* to be deleted (as witness, for instance, '(anyone) finding a small black kitten (will be rewarded)', which can't reasonably be derived from '(Anyone) who is finding a small black kitten (will be rewarded)'—see again Hudson 1973 for more discussion); but even if it didn't have problems with ordinary reduced relative clauses, it would face problems once the adverbial uses of participial clauses were taken into consideration. Extending the standard analysis to these would either mean deriving them (obligatorily) from full relative clauses, so that the relative-clause transformation as well as 'Whiz-deletion' would have to be duplicated, to cover two incompatible contexts; or it would mean deriving the adverbial and relative clauses from two different sources, by means of two unrelated rules, with the implication that the similarities between the two ranges of clause are fortuitous. On the other hand, if they are given the same source in deep structure, and this source is not the same as that for full relative clauses, then there will have to be some way of *distinguishing* it from the latter. It is hard to see how this could be done by either of the two means available in transformational grammar, namely, giving the clauses different environments (since there is no reason for giving reduced relative clauses a different relation to their noun-phrase from that of full relative clauses to their nounphrase), or using a satellite such as a 'relative-clause complementizer' for full relative clauses but not for reduced ones (since this satellite couldn't be prevented from occurring in all but the right environments). In short, there is no way in a transformational grammar of giving similar derivations to the two kinds of participial clauses, because they occur in different environments.

The last problem that I want to raise is that there are cases where different subclasses of clause occurring in the same environment may be differently affected by that environment, which means that for the same environment there may need to be more than one rule. A good example of this seems to be the relations among the 'complementizers' *whether, if, that* and zero, as in:

He didn't know whether/if/that/$\emptyset$ it was true.

It is well known that there is a restriction on '*that*-deletion', preventing it from happening before the verb—i.e. if the embedded clause is either subject or a fronted object of the main clause:

That/*$\emptyset$ it was true isn't clear/I don't believe.

What hasn't been noticed before, so far as I am aware, is that exactly the same restriction applies to the use of *if* rather than *whether:*

Whether/*if it was true isn't clear/he didn't know.

If features can be added to higher nodes, a distinction can be made between clauses introduced by *that* and *whether* on the one hand, and by zero and *if* on the other (see the feature [± mobile] of rule C.9); the former class, called in our grammar [+ mobile], are unrestricted, while the latter are restricted to occurring after the verb (by sequence rule S.4); and the internal differences in the structures of the clauses concerned are introduced by means of daughter-dependency rules sensitive to the difference between the features on the clause node (rules DD.4 and DD.6). In this way it becomes possible to bring the two sets of environmental restrictions together. In a transformational grammar, on the other hand, there is no such possibility simply because there is no way of subsuming the two internal *structural* differences under a single rule: the relation between *that* and zero is a transformational relation, while that between *whether* and *if* must, presumably, already be marked in some way in the deep structure.

It may be helpful to summarize the arguments that have been reviewed in this section and which show, it is claimed, that a grammar needs to be able to attach features to higher nodes. They all reduce to a single very general claim: that it is both desirable and, in daughter-dependency grammars, possible to separate syntagmatic relations from paradigmatic relations (using 'syntagmatic' in its usual sense, to refer to relations between constituents of the same sentence, and 'paradigmatic' in the less usual sense of Hudson 1971: 43, to refer to relations of similarity and difference among items in the language, as reflected by the syntactic features). First, some items need to be classified (paradigmatically) as both sentences and noun-phrases, without being analyzed (syntagmatically) as sentences which are daughters of noun-phrases; this is the case with gerund-clauses, which are identical in distribution to ordinary noun-phrases, and partially similar in structure, but are nevertheless still sentences. Second, it is necessary in a grammar to be able to refer to paradigmatic groupings of items which cannot be satisfactorily defined either by referring to their internal (syntagmatic) structures or by referring to their external (syntagmatic) environments, since there is no simple relation between the paradigmatic and syntagmatic groupings. In a transformational grammar it is tempting to *make* the relation simple, by creating abstract elements either within the item being classified (such as Imp) or in its immediate environment (such as Bresnan's complementizers), but this often turns out to leave the problem unsolved.

2.4. Classification of Words

It has been part of standard transformational theory for some time (since Chomsky 1965) that at least some of the terminal nodes in a syntactic structure should bear features allowing the items they represent to be both cross-classified and subclassified in the way we have seen to be necessary for clauses and phrases.

Since daughter-dependency grammars analyze *all* items in syntax, including the smallest ones, in terms of features, there is less disagreement between the two theories on the treatment of the minimal units of syntax than there is over the treatment of larger units like clauses and phrases. In particular, there is probably no disagreement in principle over the treatment of inflectional morphology: as Chomsky himself argued (1965: 174), 'the modern descriptivist reanalysis of traditional paradigmatic formulations in terms of morpheme sequences [is] an ill-advised theoretical innovation'. For instance, to take Chomsky's own example, in analyzing German nouns like *Brüder,* there is no point at all in postulating an underlying sequence of morphemes, one for the root and one each for the noun's number and case, and possibly its other properties such as its declension type. Instead, what is needed is an analysis in which all such information is given in terms of features attached (unordered, of course) to the node representing the word as a whole, and the question of how the various distinctions are reflected in the word's phonological shape can be left to be dealt with by whatever rules relate syntax and semantics to phonological form.

However, there are a number of important differences between daughter-dependency grammar and transformational grammar in their use of features on the smallest syntactic units (which for various reasons I shall assume to be words rather than morphemes). The first difference seems to be the result of analytic habits carried over from the pre-*Aspects* days, rather than a matter of principle, but it is still worth mentioning. With the possible exception of the feature-based analysis in Jacobs and Rosenbaum (1968: 109) (which transformationalists no longer defend), all transformational grammars that I know of assume that, except for bare infinitives, all verbs (in English) can be decomposed into two segmental morphemes, a root and a suffix (viz. *tense*— i.e. *past* or *present*—*ing,* or *en*). The syntax specifies verb-forms by introducing the appropriate suffix and moving it into position immediately after the verb-root. In view of Chomsky's analysis of German nouns, it is hard to see why he, and other transformational linguists, don't adopt the same approach for English verbs, to avoid the problem of postulating a *present* morpheme which is always phonologically zero (to say nothing of the problems of verbs like *took*). Instead of referring in the syntax to suffixes which couldn't be justified in a purely morphological analysis, the relevant distinctions could be made as they are in the daughter-dependency grammar in Appendix 1, by means of features on the verb word:

C.32 + verb: ± finite
C.36 + finite: ± past
C.37 − finite: ± participle
C.38 + participle: ± perfect
C.39 − perfect: ± passive

It can then be left to the rules relating syntax to phonology to spell out the phonological implications of these features.

Perhaps it was naïve to say that it is hard to see why transformational linguists don't adopt an analysis like this, since the reason is in fact clear: it would mean abandoning major parts of most current transformational grammars of English. In particular, it would no longer be possible to treat tense as a separate syntactic element, whether in Chomsky's 'Aux' analysis or in Ross and McCawley's 'higher-verb' analysis (Ross 1969a, McCawley 1971). This in turn would lead to the abandonment of Chomsky's analysis of auxiliaries, since there would be some sentences where there is no auxiliary at all—whereas treating tense as a separate element means that there will always be at least one element, tense, under Aux. Whether the higher-verb analysis could survive the loss of tense isn't clear, but in chapter 4 we shall see that there are compelling reasons for abandoning both these analyses in any case. I take it that linguists would generally agree that no syntactic analysis, least of all a bad one, can justify a bad morphological analysis.

Another difference between the two theories is in the way in which word-features are introduced. In transformational grammar, first of all the phrase-structure rules build up a structure with all the nodes, including the bottom ones, labeled with category symbols, and then the subcategorization rules add features to the bottom nodes, starting with the features mentioned by the subcategorization rules which rewrite the category symbols, and working through the remaining subcategorization rules in order. In a daughter-dependency grammar, on the other hand, there is a distinction between the classification rules, which are equivalent to subcategorization rules in that they define the possible combinations of features on a single node, and the rules which actually introduce features into structures. This means that the latter rules can introduce any feature directly, without going through the more general features on which it depends. For example, various rules (DD.1 and FA.4–7) specify what form the first verb in a clause should take—finite, participial and so on—by referring to features such as [– passive], [– perfect], [– participle] and [+ finite], but without mentioning that these features must be features of a verb. The fact that the words concerned have to be verbs follows automatically from the classification rules—the features mentioned can occur only if the same bundle of features also contains [+ verb]. Moreover, the classification rules allow all these features to combine freely either with [+ Aux] or with [– Aux], since this contrast (rule C.31) is independent of the contrasts in the form of the verb; so a rule which says e.g. that the first verb must be [+ finite] automatically allows the first verb to be either an auxiliary verb or a main verb.

It can be seen from these examples that the distinction in daughter-dependency grammar between the rules that relate features to each other (classification rules) and those that introduce features into structures allows the grammar to be flexible at a point where transformational grammar is relatively inflexible, since it allows one to refer to the form of a verb independently of its class (as auxiliary or main or whatever). It also means that the classification rules can be used as a kind of 'redundancy rule', to supply information which isn't made explicit in the other rules: any feature mentioned in the other rules can be taken to be accompanied by all the features which the classification rules say it must be accompanied by. (One advantage of the ban on disjunctions in classification rules, discussed in 2.2, is that there is never ambiguity about which features are presupposed in this way.)

An advantage that arises from the fact that features are introduced in this way is that the *position* of a feature need not be specified at the same time as its presence. As we shall see, there are several types of structure-building rule that are responsible for saying which features are present, but none of them say whereabouts in the structure the various features occur, this being done by the structure-building rules called 'sequence rules'. We shall see various advantages that come with this division of labor in the next chapter, but we can mention here that it allows a more natural analysis of the noun-phrase than the transformational approach does.

Simplifying the discussion, let us take the noun-phrases in fig. 10 as the only ones we need to generate.

	1	2	3	4
A	some boy	the boy	what boy	whose boy
B	some boys	the boys	which boy	whose boys
C	someone	he	who	who
D		they	(?)	who

Fig. 10

The columns represent distributional classes, distinguished by the intersection of the two features [± def-NP] and [± wh-phrase] (rules C.17, 18): column 1 are all [− def-NP, − wh-phrase], column 2 are [+ def-NP, − wh-phrase], column 3 are [− def-NP, + wh-phrase] (these are interrogatives), and column 4, which are relatives, are [+ def-NP, + wh-phrase]. (Interrogatives are like other indefinites in allowing *else* after them and in not occurring as partitives, and relatives are like other definites in not allowing *else* and in occurring as partitives.) The rows represent the distinction of number and the contrast between noun and pronoun.

Taking first just the top two rows, we see clearly that the determiner (*some, the, what, whose*) reflects the features [± def-NP] and [± wh-phrase], while the noun reflects the singular/plural distinction. If all noun-phrases were like this there would be no difficulty in stating the facts either in a daughter-dependency grammar or in a transformational grammar, assuming that the features concerned could simply be moved down onto the word nodes: definiteness and 'wh-ness' are located on the determiner node, and number is located on the noun node. However, the lower rows show that this isn't true of all noun-phrases, at least not on the surface, since the noun-phrases there make no surface distinction between determiner and noun. In these cases, all the distinctions are located in the same place, in the pronoun. Various ways have been suggested for treating pronouns in a transformational framework, all aiming to reflect the patterns we have just seen. In particular, Postal (1966) locates *all* the distinctions on the noun node in deep structure, and both creates the determiner node and adds some of the features to it by means of transformations, while Sommerstein (1972) seems to locate them all on the determiner node in deep structure, but renames this node 'noun' (or 'NP'?). Having created a pair of nodes, one for noun and the other for determiner, Postal is in the same position as more conservative analyses, such as Chomsky (1965: 107) and Stockwell, Schachter and Partee (1973, chaps. 4, 5), in which it is then necessary to get rid of one of the nodes in the case of pronouns. This is generally done by a rule deleting *one* (deriving *he,* for instance, from the determiner + noun sequence *he one*), though there are problems when *it* refers to a non-count noun such as *mud,* which can't be replaced by *one.* What these analyses all have in common is that determiners (or 'articles', in my analysis) and nouns are considered to be mutually exclusive categories in deep structure, occurring (if they do both occur in deep structure) in the order: determiner–noun.

The daughter-dependency approach allows a rather different and much simpler analysis, based on the possibility of introducing features into a structure without at the same time saying where they should be attached. First, a number of structure-building rules (DD.8–11) specify that any noun-phrase must contain a daughter with the feature [+ noun] and one with the feature [+ article]. (Actually, the latter feature isn't mentioned explicitly at all—it is implied by the more specific features [+ definite], [– definite] and [+ wh], in the way we explained above.)

These rules, however, don't say that [+ noun] and [+ article] must be on different nodes; whether or not this is possible is a matter for the classification rules rather than the structure-building rules to decide. When we turn to the classification rules, we find that in fact these features are compatible with each other, the relevant rules being the following ([- predicate] is the class of words other than verbs and adjectives, and in this grammar it includes both nouns and articles, as well as other kinds of word, such as prepositions):

C.40, 41 – predicate: ± article, ± noun
C.42, 43 + article: ± definite, ± wh
C.44   + noun: ± plural

Consequently, there is nothing to prevent the article and the noun from being one and the same word—as they are in the case of pronouns. Nor, of course, is there anything to *require* that they be the same word, so that full noun-phrases are also covered. If they are separate words, their order is covered by a rule (S.5) which says that articles precede nonarticles—i.e. nouns which aren't also articles. Thus the syntactic rules generate both single bundles of features, for pronouns, and pairs of bundles, for article–noun sequences. All that remains is to specify the words that can have the features concerned, and this is done in the lexicon, where all the words needed will be listed together with the syntactic features with which they are compatible. For example, *boy* will be listed as [- article, + noun] (the difference between *boy* and *boys* being handled presumably by morphological rule rather than by the lexicon), and *they* as [+ article, + definite, – wh, + noun, + plural].

There is another difference between the two theories in the way in which features are added to structures: in a daughter-dependency grammar no features are added from the lexicon, which means that there are no idiosyncratic lexical restrictions on syntax in such a grammar. In contrast, transformational grammar allows syntactic features in the lexicon which aren't present in the syntactic structure until they are brought in from the lexicon—notably rule-features and contextual features (though versions of transformational grammar have been proposed in which both of these types of feature would already be present in the deep structure, and the lexical entry would simply have to contain the same features—Chomsky 1965: 90, Lakoff 1970*b;* I shall disregard these versions of transformational grammar, as they seem to have attracted relatively little support and have few attractions). Thus, to simplify somewhat, the rules of the base generate structures containing features needed to distinguish grammatical formatives from each other plus some general features needed for distinguishing lexical formatives, and the lexicon adds to these the features which define the deep- or surface-structure environments in which individual lexical items can occur, to the extent that these can't be predicted simply from the very general features already supplied by the structure that existed before lexical insertion took place. Some of these features define deep-structure environments; these are the contextual features (strict subcategorization features and selectional features if the latter are syntactic rather than semantic). Others (rule-features) define transformations which may or may not or must apply to structures containing the lexical item in question, and thereby define surface-structure environments in which it can occur.

The daughter-dependency approach, on the other hand, generates all the features in its structures by means of syntactic rules and adds, in fact, nothing at all to the syntactic structure by lexical insertion—all that lexical insertion does is pair the syntactic structure with parts of a phonological structure and parts of a semantic one. In terms of the transformational approach we have just been considering, this means that all word-features in a daughter-dependency grammar are of the first type, the kind introduced by the base rules excluding the lexicon. This has the immediate advantage of consistency—it is no longer necessary to distinguish grammatical formatives from lexical formatives, or to distinguish between features which can be treated as part of the environment for a transformation (such as + PRO and + WH, which are used in this way in several rules in Burt 1971) and features which can't, but prevent some named transformation from applying in the environment of the lexical item in question.

Moreover, it will be recalled that no distinction is made in daughter-dependency grammar between features and categories, so there is no problem as to whether the distinction between auxiliary and main verbs is a matter of features (as Ross claims— 1969*a*) or of categories (as Chomsky has always maintained): it is a matter of features not only because that is all that the theory allows it to be but also because the descriptive facts require it to be, as we shall see in chapter 4.

The transformational approach has a number of other disadvantages, however. First, the contextual features and rule-features both have an internal structure, unlike other kinds of features. That is, whereas other features are simply arbitrary names for classes, which could easily be replaced by numbers or other arbitrary distinguishing marks without affecting the grammar in any way (though there might be problems where features are claimed to be universal—but that would be a separate problem), in the case of a contextual feature such as [+ __ NP] the material between the square brackets is not arbitrary in this sense: rather, it is a 'picture' of the environment in which the verb concerned can be fitted. Similarly, a rule-feature such as [+ rule 32] contains the number of the rule which it requires or excludes. In either case, changing the name of the feature would make nonsense, whereas with all the other types of feature the name of the feature is simply a matter of terminological convenience. Similarly, when a rule refers to a contextual feature or a rule-feature, it has to analyze its internal structure—to compare it with the context or with the number of the rule—whereas for any other type it is simply a question of whether or not a feature mentioned in a rule is the same as a feature in a structure.

Second, whatever the original intention in introducing the notion of a contextual feature or a rule-feature, these features have the effect of making surface structure give almost as much information as deep structure, since there is no mechanism for removing them once they have been inserted by the normal process of lexical insertion. For example, if a verb has a deep-structure object this will be shown even in surface structure because it will have the feature [+ __ NP]; and it will be possible to tell simply by looking at the surface structure just which transformations have taken place, since these will all be faithfully recorded among the rule-features on the verbs. This surely is against the spirit of the deep-structure/surface-structure distinction.

This seems an appropriate point to bring up another difference between daughter-dependency grammar and transformational grammar, not because it shows up a weakness of transformational grammar but simply because it is important to the understanding of daughter-dependency grammar. It is the question of how the grammar shows that a significant number of verbs all share the same *range* of possible environments. For instance, how can it show that many verbs in English can occur either with or without an object, other than by simply listing each such verb in the lexicon with both environments as possible? This is handled in transformational grammars by collapsing the two environments [– NP] and [–] into one by putting the NP in parentheses: [– (NP)]. Admittedly, this is taking perhaps unfair advantage of a facility which I have already called into question (namely, the existence of an internal structure for features of this kind), but at least it can be done in a transformational grammar. In a daughter-dependency grammar, on the other hand, it is done without any problems at all, simply by leaving the verbs in question unspecified in the lexicon for the feature which determines which of the environments is possible—in this case, verbs like *break* and *eat* would be left unspecified for [± transitive] (rule C.27), where [+ transitive] requires an object complement and [– transitive] excludes one.

Similarly, taking an example which in a standard transformational grammar would involve rule-features rather than strict subcategorization features, there are some verbs which allow as complement (*a*) a *that*-clause, (*b*) an infinitival clause, (*c*) a verbless clause, with an adjective, noun-phrase or prepositional phrase as complement:

(*a*)   I believe that he's honest.
(*b*)   I believe him to be honest.
(*c*)   I believe him honest.

Other verbs, such as *know,* allow only the first two types of environment:

- (*a*)   I know that he's honest.
- (*b*)   I know him to be honest.
- (*c*)   *I know him honest.

Yet others, such as *agree,* allow only the first type:

- (*a*)   I agree that he's honest.
- (*b*)   *I agree him to be honest.
- (*c*)   *I agree him honest.

These relations can be shown in a daughter-dependency grammar by means of two features (Rules C.24, 25), [± verbless-comp] and [± *that*-comp], with the latter depending on [– verbless-comp]. [+ verbless-comp] allows environment (*c*), [– *that*-comp] environment (*b*), and [+ *that*-comp] environment (*a*). In the lexicon, *believe* will be unspecified for both features, *know* will be specified [– verbless-comp] and *agree* will be specified [+ *that*-comp].

The last example illustrates a very general characteristic of daughter-dependency grammars, that lexical entries can be surprisingly simple (see for example all the lexical entries in section D of Appendix 1), as far as their syntactic features are concerned, since they can leave unspecified not only features which can be predicted by using the classification rules as redundancy rules, in the way described above, but also features which may be either [+] or [–]. To take a very simple instance, some nouns have to be plural, such as *scissors* and *oats;* these will be entered in the lexicon as [+ plural] (but not [+ noun], since this is predictable from [+ plural] by rule C.44). Other nouns have to be singular, such as *linguistics* (in spite of its morphology!), and these would be entered as [– plural]. Most nouns, however, would be entered simply as [+ noun], since they can be either singular or plural, and this can be left to the choice in rule C.44. Presumably this possibility is also available to transformational grammars as far as features like [± plural] are concerned, but it can be exploited more in daughter-dependency grammar because of the greater use of features.

Since the last few paragraphs have been about the advantages of having features on words rather than about the advantages of daughter-dependency grammar over transformational grammar, I should like to end this section by reviewing the criticisms I have made of transformational grammar with respect to its treatment of syntactic features. I pointed out that some aspects of current grammars of English were inconsistent with the use of features, and that if features were used consistently to show inflectional morphology, major revisions would be needed in all current transformational grammars. I don't think this amounts to a matter of principle or theory, but just of practice. What does involve questions of general theoretical principle is, first, the relation of features to categories and the rules that introduce them, and second, the relation of features to the lexicon. The first question is whether features should be introduced after, and located on, categories, and I suggested that they shouldn't, though in transformational grammar they are—it is advantageous to be able to introduce features of any degree of 'delicacy' (i.e. generality) without first identifying all the other more general features and categories on which they depend, and it is advantageous to be able to introduce features without at the same time saying where they are located. The second question is mainly to do with the use of syntactic features in the lexicon which aren't generated directly by the nonlexical syntactic rules, notably contextual features (specifically, strict subcategorization features) and rule-features. These types of features have their own problems—they have an internal structure, unlike all other types of feature in syntax (and phonology), they persist throughout the derivation, right through to surface structure, and therefore give too much information in surface structure, and they are too closely tied to the contexts and rules to which they refer, which prevents certain types of generalization from being made. However, there is also a problem in principle in that these features are present in the lexicon but not in the structures into which the lexical items are inserted: it gives the grammar an unwanted degree of flexibility, since the lexicon can do too much 'mopping up' after the ordinary syntactic rules have applied, and it makes the operation of lexical insertion more complex, since the rule has to match the contents of the lexical item not only against the features on the node where it is to be inserted but also against the environment to the left and right of that node. In a daughter-dependency grammar, on the contrary, lexical insertion is extremely simple, since it is only a question of matching features in the lexical entry against those on the node where it is to be inserted; and this is achieved without the extra cost of having rules to copy information about the environment onto the verb node, as is the case with Chomsky's proposal which leaves lexical insertion context-free (1965: 90; for criticisms see McCawley 1968*b*).

It is tempting to relate the unsatisfactory state of syntactic features in transformational grammar to the history of the model. In the early days, there were no features in transformational grammars any more than there were in the structuralist grammars such as those of Harris. It was during those days that the basic apparatus, of phrase-structure rules and transformations, was developed; and of course they were developed without regard to whether they were compatible with the use of features instead of unanalyzable category symbols. By the time of *Aspects,* it was clear that it was necessary to cross-classify and subclassify in syntax just as it was in phonology, and that meant the introduction of features into syntax. However, given the formal properties of phrase-structure rules, the only place where features could be introduced was right at the bottom of the tree, where no phrase-structure rules would have to follow them. Since the bottom of the tree is where lexical items are inserted, features thus became associated with the properties of lexical items, and were seen as an aid in the development of the lexicon as a separate element in the grammar, which was the other main development in syntactic theory taking place at the same time. This being so, it is easy to understand the initial enthusiasm of transformational linguists for the strictly lexical features which we criticized above—rule-features and contextual features. However, it is also easy to understand the reaction against such features among linguists who hoped to restrict the power of transformational grammars, since they made it too easy to mark lexical items as idiosyncratic exceptions to syntactic rules. Unfortunately, but not surprisingly, this reaction was generalized to cover syntactic features as a whole, rather than just the specifically lexical features. Meanwhile, Chomsky (to his credit) has shown the need to have features even on higher nodes in the tree; but such features are as incompatible with the basic apparatus of transformational grammar now as they were back in 1957.

3   Structure-building Rules

3.1. A General Overview

Just as the role of classification rules is to specify how features can combine with one another in a bundle attached to a single node, the role of structure-building rules is to say how nodes with different features on them can combine to form a single sentence structure. The former define 'intrabundle' (paradigmatic) relations, the latter define 'interbundle' (syntagmatic) relations. Not surprisingly, the formal properties of structure-building rules are rather more complex than those of classification rules, and there are several different types of rule to be distinguished among the structure-building rules: some to say what features should be present, others to say in what order they should come and others to provide extra information on which the order rules can operate. It may be helpful, therefore, to give a simplified view of how structure-building rules work, before going into the details of how each individual type works.

There are two types of syntagmatic relation to be shown: dependency relations and sequence relations. A dependency relation is a relation between two features where one of the features is present only when the other is present—in other words, when one depends for its presence in a structure on the presence of the other (cf. Haas's 'dependence for occurrence'—1973: 108). (Appendix 2 discusses dependency relations a little more fully.) The standard example in dependency theory is that the presence of an object noun-phrase depends on the presence in the same structure of a transitive verb, but we shall postulate other kinds of dependency relation as well, of quite a different type, namely, dependency relations between daughters and mothers, such as that between a particular form of verb and a particular set of features on the clause node. Each of these two types of dependency relations is handled by a different type of rule: the former by 'sister-dependency rules' and the latter by 'daughter-dependency rules'. In each case, what the rule does is to allow the two features (or sets of features) to occur in the same structure, with an arrow connecting them in the structure, pointing toward the dependent feature. So, to take our examples above, the sister-dependency rule for transitive verbs will allow the feature [+ transitive] and the feature [+ nominal] to occur in the same structure, with an arrow pointing from the former to the latter; and the daughter-dependency rule for clauses will allow the feature [+ sentence] to occur with [item], with an arrow pointing toward the latter. (Unfortunately this example is rather complex, since the actual features of the verb are added by a different kind of rule, to which we shall return below.)

The two kinds of rule are distinguished from each other, in terms of notation, by the position of the base of the arrow: a daughter-dependency line is attached to the *bottom* of the mother-feature, while a sister-dependency line is attached to the *top* of the feature concerned. The same distinction applies both to the rules and to the structures which they help to generate, so the rules just given and the configurations they generate are as shown in fig. 11 (they are in fact taken from the grammar in Appendix 1).

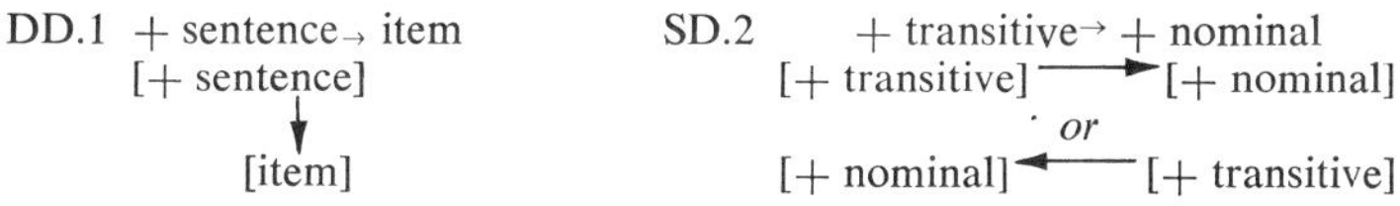

DD.1 + sentence→ item   SD.2   + transitive→ + nominal
    [+ sentence]   [+ transitive]⎯⎯→[+ nominal]
        ↓   *or*
     [item]   [+ nominal]←⎯⎯[+ transitive]

Fig. 11

To simplify the appearance of structures, the arrow will be left off the mother-daughter line (since the direction of dependence is already shown by the mother being higher than the daughter), and all arrows will be shown, in structural diagrams, as simply connecting one *bundle* of features to another, rather than picking out the individual features within the bundle. This latter simplification must be made, unfortunately, although it makes it hard to know which particular features are involved in any given dependency relation without checking back through the rules in the grammar; however, the reader will appreciate how hard it would be to show lines connecting up to individual features or sets of features. (One solution to this problem, suggested by Philipe Delcloque, is to write the number of the dependency rule concerned against the dependency arrow.)

Dependency rules leave the sequence of the elements they introduce completely unspecified—this is to be dealt with by the sequence rules, to which we shall turn shortly. This being so, there is no significance in the direction of the arrow in the rule, connecting the independent to the dependent element, provided the arrow points toward the dependent element; thus if we had no other use for the direction of the arrow we might leave it without significance, so that, for instance, the sister-dependency rule for transitive verbs could equally well be written '+ nominal ← + transitive'. However, as it happens there is another use for the direction of the arrow, since we also need to be able to define elements in terms of their dependency relation to other elements. For example, we can refer in later rules to 'the item which depends on the feature [+ sentence] as a daughter' or 'the [+ nominal] which depends as a sister on the feature [+ transitive]' (the former is the first verb in the sentence; the latter is the object, or the subject in a passive). Since the dependency rules leave 'traces' in the form of arrows in the structure (indeed, it could be said that their only function is to say where such arrows can occur), the information about dependency relations is permanently available in the structure, and can be referred to by other rules. However, there is a difference between defining a permitted dependency relation in the first place, and using a dependency relation to define some element in the way we have just been considering, so the two are kept distinct in the notation by having the arrow going from left to right in the former case, and from right to left in the latter case. The rules given above, then, can be referred to as follows in defining the dependent elements (it is never necessary, so far as I know, to define an element as

'The X on which Y depends', though it is often necessary to define one as 'the X which depends on Y'):

[+ nominal ← + transitive]   'the nominal which depends on
                              the verb's being transitive'
[item ← + S]   'the item which depends on the
                              mother's being a sentence'.

It will be seen that items defined in this way are equivalent, in transformational terms, to items defined in terms of their grammatical relations to other items in the same structure, which is the transformational way of showing grammatical functions (Chomsky 1965: 68; at the time of writing this I know too little about the new 'relational' version of transformational grammar to comment on it). By making use of dependency relations in the way I have just described, we can virtually dispense with the use of separate functional categories in daughter-dependency grammar (in contrast with the proliferating functions in other systemic grammars, notably my own earlier one, Hudson 1971). Moreover, there is an implicit claim about language structure contained in the use of this facility, since it is only items in a *dependency* relation that can be related in this way—as we shall see shortly, sequence rules as such don't leave any trace in the way of lines and arrows, so there is no simple way of referring to 'the X which follows Y'; as far as I can tell, there is no need to refer to items in this way, and the implicit claim is correct.

Sequence (or order—I shan't distinguish between the two terms) is the other type of syntagmatic relation which needs to be defined, and this is done in a daughter-dependency grammar by rules called 'sequence rules'. There are several different types of sequence rules, differing in the way in which they define the elements to which they refer—sometimes in terms of the features they have, but at other times in terms of their dependency relations or in terms of two types of property which aren't given directly in either of these ways: 'peripherality' and 'functions'. Briefly, every complement of a verb or adjective has a degree of peripherality relative to the other complements, with the least peripheral complements coming first and the most peripheral last; and to decide how peripheral the complements of a sentence are, one consults a separate set of rules, called the 'peripherality-assignment rules'. Similarly, there are three or four 'functions' which, under certain circumstances, one or more of the daughters of a sentence may have, and which make it come at the beginning of the sentence; these functions are assigned to items by rules called 'function-assignment rules', and are written in upper-case letters to keep them distinct from features: SUBJECT, TOPIC.

Sequence rules mostly take pairs of items, identified in one or another of the ways just described, and say that one of them must come before the other. In some cases, particularly where items are identified by function, a sequence rule says that they must, or may, be the same item—i.e. represented by the same node in the structure; and there are some rules which take the form of a general principle about certain items being next to each other. The rules in section K of Appendix 1 illustrate all the main types, and it will be seen from there that some types of rules are in the form of prose statements, rather than formalized rules. There would be no difficulty in principle in formalizing any of them, but there seems little point at this stage in trying to work out a formalization.

Apart from dependency rules of the two kinds described above and sequence rules, there are a number of other types of structure-building rules, of which we have already mentioned two: peripherality-assignment rules and function-assignment rules. In addition to these there is one other type: 'feature-addition rules', which take certain features or (usually) sets of features, in specified relations to the rest of the sentence, and add extra features to them—features which are compatible with them but which, if it weren't for the feature-addition rules, would simply be optional rather than obligatory. Examples of all the types of rule can be found in Appendix 1.

To recapitulate briefly, it is the dependency rules which are responsible for all the lines in a structure: daughter-dependency rules for lines between mothers and daughters (i.e. for vertical or diagonal lines) and sister-dependency rules for lines between sisters (horizontal lines). All the other types of rule are responsible either for the presence of extra labels (functions in function-assignment rules, features in feature-addition rules) or for the order of elements, from left to right across the structure (in sequence rules, in conjunction with peripherality-assignment rules).

3.2. Daughter-dependency Rules

The aim of this section is to compare daughter-dependency rules with their counterparts in transformational grammar, phrase-structure rules. These two kinds of rule are comparable in that they are both responsible for the presence of daughters within mothers—it is such a rule, for example, that says that a noun-phrase has a noun inside it as a daughter. There are important differences between them too, however, as we shall see, and it can be shown, I believe, that these differences are to the advantage of daughter-dependency grammar. In some cases they follow automatically from other characteristics of the two theories —in particular, from the presence in daughter-dependency grammar of features on higher nodes, which we justified in the previous chapter. In others, they have advantages for daughter-dependency grammar over and above the advantages accruing from the use of features on higher nodes.

The first point to notice, before we start considering the differences between phrase-structure rules and daughter-dependency rules, is that they can both be seen as members of a more general class of rules, which we can call 'daughter-dependency rules', since their role is precisely to define dependency relations between mothers and daughters. Take as an example of a phrase-structure rule the first one in many transformational grammars (excluding some adverbials):

S → (Pre-S) NP Aux VP (Time)

Seen as a daughter-dependency rule, this rule states, for example, that Aux can occur as a daughter only if its mother bears the label S, and similarly for VP and Time and Pre-S: these elements show a daughter-dependency relation to their mother, the S, in that they are allowed to occur only if they have S as mother. Of course, there are problems in formulating dependency relations, but these are not unique to the idea of daughter-dependency rules. For one thing, there may be elements like the NP in this rule which are in fact allowed to occur as daughters of other kinds of mother—such as VP; in such cases it clearly isn't true to say that the daughter depends on the mother in quite the way described above, and one has to make the dependency specific to the structure in hand: the subject NP depends on the mother S in that in this particular structure the former occurs only by virtue of the latter—although in other structures it may occur by virtue of some other kind of mother. And for another problem, dependency works in both directions where a daughter is obligatory, such as NP, Aux and VP, since S can't occur without its obligatory daughters any more than they can occur without it. In our grammar, as in transformational grammars, the distinction is made in terms of optional and obligatory dependencies, but it could be made in terms of unilateral versus reciprocal dependencies. Whether there is an issue of principle here I don't know.

Within this larger class of 'daughter-dependency rules', which includes both phrase-structure rules and the particular kind of daughter-dependency rule used in daughter-dependency grammar, we can then identify the properties of the two subtypes which distinguish them from one another (using the term 'daughter-dependency rule' just for the subtype). The following list summarizes the differences:

1. Mothers are defined in terms of unitary categories in phrase-structure rules, but in terms of features in daughter-dependency grammars.
2. Daughters are introduced two or more at a time in phrase-structure rules, but one at a time in daughter-dependency rules.
3. Daughters are introduced in a particular sequence in phrase-structure rules, but not in daughter-dependency rules.
4. Double-motherhood is forbidden (in practice) in phrase-structure rules, but not in daughter-dependency rules.

5. Discontinuities are forbidden in phrase-structure rules, but not in daughter-dependency rules.
6. Phrase-structure rules introduce *all* daughters of a given mother, but daughter-dependency rules introduce only some of the daughters, leaving some to be introduced by sister-dependency rules.

We shall now consider these differences in turn.

First: categories or features for defining the mother? This difference follows automatically from the fact that mothers have no features in transformational grammar, and that they have *only* features in daughter-dependency grammar. The reasons for this difference have already been discussed, in 2.3. The nearest one could get to the phrase-structure rule quoted above would be a daughter-dependency rule with [+ sentence] on the left. However, in practice this rule wouldn't be possible, since other features occur in bundles with [+ sentence], and not all of them are compatible with the same range of daughters—for example, different pre-sentence elements and different auxiliaries are possible according to whether the sentence is a gerund-clause [+ sentence, + phrase, + nominal] or a main interrogative [+ sentence, − phrase, − nominal, − optative, + moody, + interrogative]. (Actually the position would be more complex than this, since it isn't the daughters but the *grand*daughters that are restricted in this way.) This is the reason why features on higher nodes aren't compatible with phrase-structure rules, as we saw in the first chapter: different daughters are sensitive to the presence on the mother of different features. As we shall see below, the use of features on higher nodes has far-reaching consequences.

Second: daughters introduced all together or one at a time? This difference follows more or less directly from the first, since if different daughters are sensitive to the presence of different features, we shall naturally need different rules for different daughters, relating them to different features of the mother. The question then is simply how much similarity there is among the daughters in the mother-features to which they are sensitive. It might turn out that for most mothers a single rule, referring to just one set of mother-features, could be written to account for the presence of most of its daughters, leaving just a few oddities (like 'complementizers' and 'pre-sentences') to be added by other rules. At least as far as the grammar in Appendix 1 is concerned, however, there seems to be relatively *little* similarity among daughters in the mother-features to which they are sensitive, though it may be that extending the grammar in some ways —say, to cover adverbials—would change the picture. It should also be borne in mind that part of the reason for the lack of similarity among daughter-dependency rules in our grammar is that a good number of daughters aren't introduced in this way, but by means of sister-dependency rules, so there aren't so very many daughter-dependency rules which *could* show similarities. Whatever the reason for the lack of generalizable daughter-dependency relations, there are no cases in our grammar where two daughter-dependency rules could be merged into a single one, so we can assume, for the time being at least, that each rule introduces just one daughter *as a matter of principle*.

Third: daughters ordered or not by the rules that introduce them? It has generally been assumed that phrase-structure rules order the elements that they introduce, although objections have been raised by G. Hudson (1972) and Sanders (1970, 1975), who suggest that deep structure might be unordered. The assumption that elements are ordered at the same time that they are introduced is a natural one, given that elements are introduced in groups, rather than one at a time. However, it is clear that this is using one rule to show two quite different kinds of relation: the dependency relations between mothers and daughters, and the sequence relations between sisters. Killing two birds with one stone is good provided the stone doesn't fall on another bird and wake it up—requiring a further stone to bring *it* down. This seems to be the case with the ordering of elements by phrase-structure rules: when *some* surface ordering is accounted for in this way it becomes necessary to have reordering transformations, since in some cases the order imposed by the phrase-structure rules is different from the surface order. This is always the case when the same element, in the same daughter-dependency relation to its mother, can occur in more than one order relative

to its sisters—as, for example, with adverbials in clause structure. Given that, say, 'Time' is introduced by the phrase-structure
rule for S and that elements introduced by phrase-structure rules
can't be left unordered, there is no way of generating structures
by phrase-structure rule alone in which Time is in all the places
where it can appear in the surface—at the start of the clause, at
its end, and in various places in the middle. (Adding a few extra
occurrences of 'Time' to the phrase-structure rule for S wouldn't
help, since we should then have the problem of making sure that
only one of them was actually added.) Consequently one has to
choose some order as the basic one—a choice, incidentally,
which is fairly arbitrary as far as elements like 'Time' are concerned—and impose that order by means of the phrase-structure
rules, leaving various other orders to be introduced by transformation.

In contrast, there is no temptation at all to let daughter-dependency rules order the daughters as they introduce them, since
the daughters are introduced one at a time. To make such rules
impose order would be quite difficult, and would in any case
probably amount to having a separate set of rules for ordering
elements, like our sequence rules. Moreover, where there are no
restrictions on the order of elements, all the grammar need do is
state their daughter-dependency relations, and say nothing about
their positions, since every position will be permissible (where
position is partly free, as with adverbials in English, some positions can be ruled out by other rules, in particular by the sequence rule preferring dependent sisters to be as close as possible
to one another—rule S.11—and it may still be unnecessary to
say anything specifically about the position of the more or less
free elements).

This difference between phrase-structure rules and daughter-
dependency rules goes even further than I have been assuming
so far: daughter-dependency rules don't even tell you which elements are *separate* from each other. All a daughter-dependency
rule of the form 'X⌐ Y' tells you is that somewhere among the
daughters of X must be one with the feature Y; so if there are two
rules which both apply to the same mother and each introduces

a different feature, there is nothing to stop both features from being features of the same daughter. We have already seen (in 2.4) that this can be an advantage in dealing with constructions like the noun-phrase, where [+ article] and [+ noun], and all the features that each of them brings with it, may be combined on a single node, as for pronouns, or located on separate nodes, as for ordinary article-plus-noun sequences.

Fourth: double-motherhood forbidden or permitted? By 'double-motherhood' I mean the state of having two mothers, a state in which items may be in in a daughter-dependency grammar but not in a transformational grammar. Sampson has suggested (1975) that there is no reason why transformational grammar *shouldn't* allow double-motherhood, if phrase-structure rules are taken as conditions on well-formedness, since an NP node can satisfy the node-admissibility conditions on more than one mother node at the same time without any change in the way node-admissibility conditions are formulated. This would make a wide range of transformations which depend on two NPs being identical unnecessary in the grammar, at least to the extent that one of the two identical NPs would otherwise need deleting. However, attractive though this proposal is, it raises other problems. For instance, if an NP can have two mothers, why shouldn't, say, a preposition? But if this is allowed, then a special transformation will be needed for 'untying' the preposition from one of its deep-structure mothers and then copying it under that mother—otherwise surface structures will result in which a single preposition has two mothers, which Sampson surely wouldn't want. Whatever the merits of Sampson's suggestion, the fact remains that it has in practice always been assumed by transformationalists that double-motherhood is illegitimate—as it clearly is if phrase-structure rules are interpreted, as they usually have been, as operations rather than conditions. In contrast, as I shall now explain, daughter-dependency grammars generate double-motherhood configurations quite easily.

What is needed to give a single item two mothers is, first, rules defining the conditions on mother-daughter combinations (i.e. daughter-dependency rules) and second, what Sampson's proposal lacks, a way of defining the conditions under which an item can have two mothers. This is provided in daughter-dependency grammars by the function-assignment rules, which we shall discuss in some detail in 3.6 and 3.8 below, but which can be briefly said to define the conditions concerned as 'An item can have two mothers if, and only if, it satisfies the conditions for being assigned one of the functions SCENE-SETTER, TOPIC or SUBJECT in the higher and also for being a daughter of the lower'. Whatever the actual mechanism—and a fuller explanation is obviously needed—the effect is to allow constructions involving *raising* to be handled in terms of double-motherhood. For example, if a sentence like 'John seems to have hiccoughs' is analyzed as having a 'split subject', with *John* as subject not only of the main clause but also of the subordinate one, this can be shown by treating *John* as having two mothers—the main clauses and the subordinate clause. The structure diagram looks roughly like fig. 12.

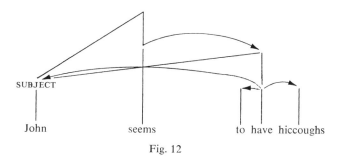

SUBJECT

John   seems   to have hiccoughs

Fig. 12

Diagrams like this can't be generated by phrase-structure rules because of a combination of the characteristics already discussed: daughters are introduced all together, and they are ordered as they are introduced, so it is assumed that they are ordered relative to one another, and never relative to some element outside the mother—in other words, they are never ordered relative to an element other than one of their own sisters. The argument then continues as follows: since this is a characteristic of the structures generated by phrase-structure rules (namely, that they don't contain instances of double-motherhood), and since it is assumed that all the syntactic structures in a derivation have the same formal properties (they are 'phrase-markers'), it follows that *no* structures in a derivation should show double-motherhood. Consequently, if we want to analyze a sentence as involving some kind of raising, we have to show one of the relevant mother-daughter links in one structure, and the other in another structure—but never both in one. In other words, the transformation that (say) raises a subject of one clause to act as object of a higher clause has to destroy the link within the lower clause in order to be able to show the one in the higher clause.

Not being able to show double-motherhood is a nuisance for transformational grammar, because it brings in the need for *global rules*. Lakoff (1970*a*: 628, quoting Andrews) points out that in classical Greek participles agree in number, gender and case with their subjects, even if the latter have been raised into the structure of a higher clause and have there taken on some function which requires a case such as dative. The problem is that at the stage in the derivation where the case of the subject can be specified, its connection with the embedded clause (its source) has been lost, so the rules for assigning case and so on to the participle have to refer to the NP which was the subject of the participle at an earlier stage. This makes the agreement rules global, and it is generally agreed that allowing global rules in a transformational grammar adds immensely to the power of the grammar, which is bad. It is hard to see any way around this problem in transformational grammar, but in a daughter-dependency grammar there is no problem, since the structure shows *both* allegiances of the raised subject within the same structure. The case of the subject will be determined by its place in the higher clause, and then the agreement rules will simply copy this case onto the participle. To make matters worse for transformational grammar, it isn't even clear that global rules are *possible* in this framework, since a rule like the Greek agreement rule has to be able to identify some NP in a late structure with a particular NP in an early structure—but there is no obvious way of doing so. One possibility, suggested by Baker and Brame (1972:

52), is to assign an index number to every NP as it gets introduced, so that each NP will have a constant number wherever it turns up in the course of the derivation, even if it gets moved by a transformation. They don't say how indices should be assigned, however, or whether they would allow indices to be assigned to new NP nodes that were created in the course of a derivation—by conjunction-reduction, for example. Until the implications of this suggestion have been worked out in detail, it seems best to leave completely open the question of whether global rules are in fact compatible with the transformational framework. It may turn out that global rules are *necessary but neither desirable nor possible;* if so the question is whether the problems aren't in fact created by the transformational framework, rather than by the facts of language.

Fifth: discontinuity forbidden or permitted? In a transformational grammar, discontinuity is forbidden for the same reasons as double-motherhood: it would require a daughter of one mother being ordered with respect to daughters of a different mother, which can't be done by phrase-structure rules. Once again, since discontinuities aren't found in the structures generated by phrase-structure rules, they are excluded in principle from *all* syntactic structures; so if a transformation introduces a discontinuity it shows it only indirectly in the structures generated, by comparing structures at different stages in the derivation. For instance, after extraposition has taken place the structure shows no particular connection between the extraposed S node and the rest of the NP out of which it has been moved; the fact that this NP is discontinuous can be seen only by comparing early stages in the derivation with stages after extraposition has taken place. In a daughter-dependency grammar, on the other hand, discontinuities are shown *as such* in the syntactic structure, where lines from different mothers are allowed to cross over, as they did in the subject-raising example given above. Moreover, all cases of discontinuity are handled in daughter-dependency grammar as cases of raising into a preexisting higher structure (as we shall see below, many of the constructions which transformationalists consider to involve discontinuities can be analyzed without any kind of discontinuity in a daughter-dependency grammar). This rules out analyses like Ross's analysis of wh-movement in questions and relative clauses (reported in Stockwell, Schachter and Partee 1973, chap. 8, section 9), which strikes me as a cheat: instead of simply moving the 'wh'-element to the head of the sentence, the wh-movement transformation Chomsky-adjoins it to the whole of the sentence, creating a new sentence node to dominate the moved element plus the rest of the original sentence—thereby changing the dependency relations drastically, and moving the wh-element up into a structure which didn't exist before. The only motivation for this analysis is to make Ross's (1967) 'coordinate structure constraint' work, since otherwise wh-elements wouldn't be moved at all if they were subject, and sentences like *'Who and John came?' wouldn't be ruled out by the constraint that rules out *'Who did you see and John?'. An analysis like this, whose sole justification is that it patches up some rule which would otherwise not work, is impossible in principle in a daughter-dependency grammar, since elements can only be raised into structures that already exist (and, moreover, in only a very limited number of positions, as we shall see in 3.8).

It should be explained, in connection with discontinuities, that many constructions which are treated in transformational grammars as instances of discontinuity are treated differently in daughter-dependency grammar, by means of *sister*-dependency rules relating sisters which have other elements separating them. This is how extraposition is handled, for example: the expletive *it* and the extraposed clause are treated as sisters, as in the transformational analysis, but as sisters in the structure of the main clause, rather than in the structure of a (discontinuous) noun-phrase. In other words, they are sisters not only of each other but also of the main clause's other daughters, such as its verb. (The *it* is introduced by an optional sister-dependency rule, SD.16, applying to certain embedded clauses.) This analysis has the advantage that it can easily be extended to cover extraposition of noun-phrases like 'the way he keeps on talking about her', which can be extraposed in sentences like 'It's funny the way he keeps on talking about her', as we saw in 2.3. We shall see other examples of the use of sister-dependency between nonadjacent elements in the next section; all of these would be treated in transformational grammar as instances of discontinuity.

Sixth: all or only some of daughters introduced by daughter-dependency rule or phrase-structure rule? Transformational grammar introduces all daughters in the same way, by phrase-structure rule, but daughter-dependency grammar introduces some in this way and others by means of sister-dependency rules. In particular, daughter-dependency grammar introduces all the complements of the predicate by means of sister-dependency rules, whereas transformational grammar introduces them all by phrase-structure rules for a specially created node, **VP**. We shall be considering the advantages of this distinction further in the next section, but we can point to one advantage here: that dependency relations are located, in the structures that are generated, where they are relevant. If the features of the clause are restricted to showing distributional differences between clauses —as they are in daughter-dependency grammar—then the fact is that the types of complement that the verb has are never relevant to the distributional class of the clause. On the other hand, the kind of verb (or more precisely, the type of item acting as the clause's first 'predicate') *is* relevant to the clause's distributional class, and is shown by daughter-dependency rules, while complements are introduced by sister-dependency rules. This gives the kind of 'bird's leg' appearance typical of daughter-dependency structure diagrams, with a single vertical line relating the clause to the verb and then a number of horizontal lines linking the verb to its complements.

We can finish this section by pointing out an incidental advantage of the bird's leg analysis: it explains, or at least helps to explain, why so many languages have verbs which inflect for contrasts like mood and tense. Consider an alternative arrangement (which may well be actually found), with two separate words in the sentence, one showing mood and so on—in other words, contrasts relevant to the class of the clause—and the other defining the number of complements permitted—in other words, the verb. In such a language, two daughter-dependency rules are needed, one for the marker of the clause's class, and one for the verb; and sentences would be one word longer than in English, other things being equal. Compared with this, the arrangement we have in English gets away with just one daughter-dependency rule, which introduces an item with features like [+ finite], and the classification rules tell us that any item with features like this must have other features as well, which determine the number and type of complements. Of the two arrangements, the English one is simpler in the syntax, though probably more complex in the morphology (the other one could get away without any inflectional morphology at all), so one might expect both to occur. However, a grammar should reveal the advantages and disadvantages of each, as I believe daughter-dependency grammar does. By this criterion, transformational grammars are inadequate, since the connection between the verb and the markers of clause classes (viz. the complementizers) is accidental: the complementizers all start off separate from the verb of the complement-clause, and those like -ING which get attached to this verb only get attached to it by transformations, so presumably it would be pure gain for a language to *lose* these transformations and keep the complementizers where they are in deep structure. As I have suggested, however, there are gains as well as losses in having the 'complementizers' merged with the verb (and not with any other element, incidentally), so a transformational grammar ought to show the advantages—which it doesn't. (I have been deliberately vague in this paragraph in referring to 'the verb'; in terms of the analysis in chapter 4, I have been consistent, in referring always to the first verb, whether this is an auxiliary or a main verb, but in terms of most transformational analyses I have been ignoring the distinction between auxiliaries, which receive the complementizer suffixes, and main verbs, which define the type and number of complements. The latter analysis makes the connection between complementizers and verbs even more accidental and remote than I have suggested.)

3.3. Sister-dependency Rules

There is no single equivalent of sister-dependency rules in a transformational grammar, so we shall have to consider connections in this section between sister-dependency rules and various aspects of transformational grammar. As we have just seen, all the *elements* which are introduced in a daughter-dependency grammar by sister-dependency rules are introduced in a transformational grammar by phrase-structure rules (though Chafe—1970: 102—has suggested an alternative version of transformational grammar which is more similar in this respect to daughter-dependency grammar). However, much of the *information* conveyed by sister-dependency rules is located, in a transformational grammar, in the strict subcategorization features in the lexicon, and it is these which define the dependency relations between verbs and their complements. Moreover, it is the lexical insertion which takes account of the strict subcategorization features in building up a sentence structure, so this too is involved in the comparison between sister-dependency rules and the transformational equivalents. Since the comparison has to be more diffuse in this section, it isn't feasible to start with a neat checklist of points of difference as we did in the last section. However, we shall be focusing on differences and trying once again to show the superiority of daughter-dependency grammar for each difference.

The first difference is that dependency relations between sisters aren't shown at all in the structures generated by a transformational grammar (this is one of Robinson's major criticisms of transformational grammar as opposed to dependency grammar —1970). (As Keith Brown has pointed out to me, the earliest grammars based on 'I.C. analysis', such as Nida 1960, *do* show dependency relations between sisters in their structures.) Instead of showing dependency relations in structures, as is done in both daughter-dependency grammar and dependency grammar, transformational grammar shows them in the rules and the lexicon. To take a simple example, the dependence of the object on the verb is shown by making the latter obligatory and the former optional, which has the effect of predicting that the object won't occur without a verb; and the dependence of the object on the verb belonging to a particular class ('transitive') is shown by giving all the verbs in that class the strict subcategorization feature which allows them to be followed by an object. As far as the structures generated are concerned, however, there is no difference at all between the status of the verb and that of the object —they are both simply daughters of VP. A clear demonstration of the superiority of the daughter-dependency approach would be evidence that rules in the grammar need to be able to refer to the sister-sister dependency relations, which they clearly couldn't do in a transformational grammar. There is a very tentative sequence rule in our grammar (S.11) which does this, requiring the dependent element to follow the one on which it depends; but this rule is so tentative that it can't be taken as evidence for the daughter-dependency approach. (Another such rule is proposed in Hudson 1976*b,* but it is too complex to discuss here.)

What *does* favor this approach, at least in comparison with transformational grammar, is that it shows sister-sister dependencies only once each, whereas in a transformational grammar they are shown *twice* in the grammar (and not at all in the structures generated). This is so because the information about dependencies which is given in the phrase-structure rules, as I explained above (by means of the distinction between obligatory and optional constituents), is *also* given in the strict subcategorization features: the elements which are shown as optional are the ones that are treated as 'environment' in the strict subcategorization features, and vice versa. The problem with this duplication of information, as in other such cases, is not so much that it is uneconomical—it is hard to see how it could be avoided in a transformational grammar, so there is no simpler, more economical alternative to be preferred—but rather that it denies any connection between the two aspects of the grammar that reflect the same facts. That is, the grammar doesn't show that it *has* to be the obligatory element (the verb) which is strictly subcategorized, rather than, say, the NP; and it would have been just as easy to write a grammar if the only obligatory element in the VP had been an NP—it would still be possible to strictly subcategorize verbs rather than NPs. In a daughter-dependency grammar this is not so, since the dependencies between verbs and their complements are shown only once and it is the rules which reflect these dependencies which actually introduce 'optional' elements.

The problem in the last paragraph arose from the fact that in a transformational grammar there are two separate operations, one for creating structures containing verbs and their complements, and another for selecting particular verbs to fit into particular preformed structures. This characteristic of transformational grammar has other undesirable consequences too. First, it makes it hard to generate permitted combinations of complements, since this has to be done without distinguishing different subclasses of verb. This is why we find a rule as complicated and unrevealing as the following in *Aspects* (Chomsky 1965: 107):

$$VP \rightarrow \left\{ \begin{array}{l} \text{copula predicate} \\ V \left\{ \begin{array}{l} \text{(NP) (Prep-phrase) (Prep-phrase) (manner)} \\ S' \\ \text{predicate} \end{array} \right\} \end{array} \right\}$$

This rule makes it coincidental, for example, that 'predicate' occurs twice; it fails to treat the copula *be* as a verb (as it should be treated—see the arguments in chapter 4), and 'predicate' is in any case an illegitimate cover-term for a range of categories such as adjective, prepositional phrase and noun-phrase, so if it were dispensed with the rule would look even worse. If a distinction were made between verbs that do and those that don't take a 'predicate' (in Chomsky's sense), the rule could be simplified, allowing 'predicates' with one kind of verb, and not with the other. The second undesirable consequence of reflecting dependencies both in the phrase-structure rules and in the lexicon is that it makes lexical insertion harder: since (in the normal analysis) the category 'verb' is undifferentiated when lexical insertion takes place, all the distinctions among different types of verb, occurring in different contexts, must be given in the lexicon, which means that the lexical-insertion rule has to be able to match the contents of the strict subcategorization features of a verb against the structure into which it is to be inserted—a very much more complex operation than simply matching the features in the lexical entry against those already on the verb node, as in daughter-dependency grammar. (It also has undesirable implica-

tions for the formal properties of features, since strict subcategorization features have to have an internal structure—see 2.4.)
In sum, then, transformational grammar creates problems by
reflecting dependencies between verbs and their complements at
two separate places in the grammar.

A further advantage of the daughter-dependency approach is
that it merges the two operations of lexical selection of a verb
and the insertion of complementizers into one, since the sister-
dependency rules for verbs can define the classes of clause which
they take as complements sufficiently precisely to predict which
'complementizer' they need. For instance, a daughter-dependency grammar shows that *probable* allows only a *that*-clause as
complement (whereas *likely* allows either a *that*-clause or an infinitival clause) by classifying *probable* in the lexicon as [– infin-
comp] (see Appendix 1, section D) and having a sister-dependency rule (SD.9):

– infin-comp → + nominal, – optative, – interrogative.

This rule allows a clause as complement with *probable,* but defines it at the same time as a *that*-clause (this being the kind of
clause defined as [+ nominal, – optative, – interrogative]—see
section B of Appendix 1). On the other hand, for *likely* it specifies the features [– verb, + epistemic], which allows it to have
either the feature [– infin-comp] (rule C.26) or the feature
[+ infin-comp]. The former feature allows it to have a *that*-clause,
just as for *probable,* and the latter allows an infinitival complement (by sister-dependency rule SD.8). In contrast, a transformational grammar has first of all to allow *likely* and *probable* to
have S as a complement (maybe embedded within NP—which
raises problems for strict subcategoziration, since the S is then
not a sister but a niece of the adjective), and then to add features
to them to show which complementizers each of them allows,
these being added by transformation (in the standard theory,
though not in Bresnan's analysis). As far as this analysis is concerned, it should be noticed that no connection is made between
the strict subcategorization feature which allows the S, and the
rule-features which allow it to have complementizers—whereas

of course any lexical item that allows S as complement must also have rule-features allowing complementizers to be inserted, and vice versa.

We can now consider a problem raised by the way in which phrase-structure rules are used to show dependencies between sisters. The problem is that there are two ways in which such dependencies can be shown in a transformational grammar, and there is no way of choosing between them. This can easily be illustrated by looking at the history of the rule for Aux. In *Syntactic Structures* (Chomsky 1957: 39) the rule was this:

Aux → C(M) (have + *en*) (be + *ing*) (be + *en*)

whereas in Burt (1971: 243) it is like this:

Aux → tense + (M) + (Perf) + (Prog) + (Pass),

with extra rules for rewriting Perf and so on, such as

Perf → have + *en*.

Both grammars show a dependency between *have* and *en* (and so on for the other auxiliaries), but they do it in different ways: one simply by putting brackets around the two elements to show that if one occurs so must the other, and the other by postulating an intermediate constituent, 'Perf'. It is hard to imagine any way of deciding between these two analyses on empirical grounds, and both are legitimate uses of the formal apparatus of transformational grammar. Similarly, one thinks of the changes in the fortunes of the VP constituent, whose main function is to bring together the verb and the elements that depend on it, though here the alternative to having VP seems to be an analysis which shows dependencies simply through strict subcategorization (Fillmore 1968, McCawley 1970). These problems are avoided in daughter-dependency grammar by the use of sister-dependency rules to show all dependencies and in general by having much less constituent structure (Hudson 1967). The relative 'flatness' of daughter-dependency structures is largely due to the fact that elements introduced by daughter-dependency rules have to be daughters (not granddaughters) of the higher nodes, and any elements depending on them as sisters have to be daughters of these same higher nodes. In particular, the verb is introduced by a daughter-dependency rule for the clause, which immediately rules out both the VP node and the Aux node (for reasons which we shall see in chapter 4); and all the complements of the verb must also be daughters of the clause. As for the grouping of *have* and *en* into a single constituent, we shall be rejecting the analysis on which this problem rests in chapter 4, so the problem doesn't arise. All we need do is show a sister-dependency between the verb *have* and the perfect participle following it (by rule SD.12).

For some constructions, then, there are too many ways in which the dependencies concerned can be shown in a transformational grammar. On the other hand, there is at least one construction for which there is *no* way of showing the dependencies, so far as I can see. This is the kind of sentence in which *each* floats free, as an adverb, as in 'The competitors must each burst three balloons'. This *each* depends on there being a plural noun-phrase before it, like *the competitors* in the above sentence. It is tempting in a transformational grammar to show this dependence by deriving the adverb *each* from a deep-structure determiner (or pronoun) preceding the noun-phrase on which it depends; some way could no doubt then be found to prevent it from occurring before a singular noun-phrase. The determiner analysis has to be rejected immediately, since the rule for determiner *each* is that it can only occur in *singular* noun-phrases (*each competitor* but not **each competitors*). The pronoun analysis is more attractive, since *each of the competitors* is possible, but **each of the competitor* isn't; but there are problems for this analysis too, since the plural noun-phrase on which adverb *each* depends can be indefinite, but that which can follow pronoun *each* can't:

Some competitors will each burst three balloons.
*Each of some competitors will burst three balloons.

Moreover, there is the problem of changing a pronoun (or however *each* is labeled) into an adverb, to be placed by the ordinary rules for adverbs like *soon*. It seems, then, that there is no way in which *each* can be put into the same underlying constituent as the plural noun-phrase on which it depends; and to the extent that dependencies can be shown, in a transformational grammar, only between sisters within the same mother, it follows that the dependence of *each* on *some competitors* can't be shown. To make matters worse, *each* can also depend on another element in addition to the plural noun-phrase, since it can follow an indefinite noun-phrase:

The competitors must burst three balloons each.
*The competitors must burst the three balloons each.
The competitors must burst a balloon each.

This *each* depends for its presence on the plurality of the subject noun-phrase, but for its position it depends on the indefiniteness of the second noun-phrase. On the other hand, to be fair to transformational grammar, this is less of a problem than the dependence of *each* on *some competitors,* since it presumably just means that there is a transformation for moving *each* after a noun-phrase which can be sensitive to the latter's definiteness. (For more discussion of the syntax of *each,* see Hudson 1970.)

The last advantage of sister-dependency rules is that, like daughter-dependency rules, they leave sequence unspecified. This has the advantage that the sequence of complements can be stated by means of general rules covering other elements as well as verb-complements—for example, the position of the agentive *by*-phrase (introduced by sister-dependency rule SD.3) is determined by the general rules for the position of prepositional phrases: prepositional phrases follow noun-phrases. (This also covers the position of *to*-phrases.) Similarly, another advantage is that the general rules can define the possible orderings of complements without referring to the position of the verb among the complements; this can then be specified by a separate rule which will probably vary more from language to language than the ones governing the order of complements do—some languages put the verb before all the complements (VSO), others after all of them (SOV), and others straight after the subject (SVO)—but in nearly all languages the order of subject and object is the same. More discussion of these questions will be found in 3.7 below.

3.4. Feature-addition Rules

Apart from the two types of dependency rules, which we have now discussed, the main type of structure-building rule in a daughter-dependency grammar is the type called 'sequence rules', whose job it is to put the elements introduced by the dependency rules into the right order. However, before we can discuss these rules we shall have to deal with a number of other, rather subordinate, types of rule, the first of which is the type called 'feature-addition rules'.

Feature-addition rules don't seem to bring any extra advantages to a grammar, so all I shall do in this section is explain why they are necessary and what they are. Briefly, a feature-addition rule has the form '[X]: Y', where X and Y are sets of features, and a bundle containing X must also contain Y, unless there are structural reasons why it shouldn't. [X] can be thought of as the 'input' to the rule, and the output will be a bundle of features containing both X and Y. The rule applies whenever [X] occurs and no other rules have applied to the same bundle of features requiring it to contain other features which are incompatible with Y (incompatible, that is, with respect to the classification rules). An example will help to make this clear.

The simplest feature-addition rule in Appendix 1 is rule FA.11, which is responsible for making sure that the top node in the structure carries features appropriate to a main clause:

FA.11   [item]: − nominal, + moody.

The features [− nominal, + moody] are sufficient to define the class of main clauses (see section B of Appendix 1), so this rule, whenever it applies, guarantees that the item to which it applies will be a main clause. However, it clearly mustn't apply to most items, and it is prevented from doing so by the fact that every item except the top one in the structure will already have some of its features specified by the dependency rule (or rules) which introduced it; and in most cases these features will be incompatible with [− nominal, + moody].

In one respect this rule is untypical of feature-addition rules:

it has a very simple input, namely, [item]. There is only one other rule in our grammar with an input as simple as this: FA.7, which says that any verb is finite, unless there are reasons for it being otherwise. (This rule simplifies the grammar by not requiring us to have separate rules for all the different contexts in which finite verbs are found—they are treated simply as what is left over after all the contexts requiring a nonfinite verb have been taken out.) All the remaining feature-addition rules have as input a set of features which include an arrow showing a daughter-dependency relation. For example, the input to rule FA.4 is [item_← + sentence, + phrase, + nominal], meaning 'The item which depends, as a daughter, on the feature [+ sentence], when this is combined with [+ phrase, + nominal]'. The features [+ sentence, + phrase, + nominal], it will be recalled, define the class of gerund-clauses, and the daughter-dependency rule '+ S_→ item' (DD.1) introduces the 'predicate', which may be a verb, an adjective, a prepositional phrase, or a noun-phrase. Accordingly, the input to feature-addition rule FA.4 defines the verb in a gerund-clause—or more precisely the *first* verb in such a clause, since all the following ones are introduced by sister-dependency rules, as we shall see in chapter 4. Given this input, the rule tells us that the verb has to be an *ing*-form. Similarly, rules FA.1 to FA.6 run through the various other types of clause and specify the type of 'predicate' they need. Rules FA.8 to FA.10 do the same for 'complementizers', relating the type of complementizer to the type of clause containing it.

Why are feature-addition rules needed? First, because some constraints are put on features by the *absence* of any context at all, and this clearly can't be expressed in terms of daughter-dependency rules, precisely because there would be no mother to refer to in the rule. This explains the need for the first rule we discussed. (It could, in fact, be argued that this rule is both wrong and unnecessary, since we don't always use complete sentences when we talk, as in answers to questions, and in any case to the extent that there is pressure on us to use complete main clauses, it's a pragmatic pressure, not a syntactic one. If this is so, the first rule is unnecessary, and maybe this reason for having feature-addition rules disappears.) As for the other rules, feature-addition rules are needed to establish connections between the features of mothers and those of daughters when these involve a range of features on some daughter (such as the 'predicate') varying according to a range of features on the mother. It is easier to express this kind of relationship in terms of feature-addition rules than in terms of the alternative, daughter-dependency rules, since one can introduce the daughter concerned by means of a single daughter-dependency rule, and then use that daughter-dependency rule to *define* the daughter whose features vary with the features of the mother.

3.5. Peripherality-assignment Rules

The three types of structure-building rule that we have considered so far (two kinds of dependency rule and feature-addition rules) have been responsible for predicting which features will occur within the structure of some item, given the features that it (the mother) has. We now turn toward the rules that are responsible for saying how these features will be distributed among the item's daughters—that is, how many daughters there will be, what features they must have and in what order they come. Their task reduces, in effect, to that of ordering the features from left to right, with the possibility that some of them will be put into bundles together, to be attached to the same node. Peripherality-assignment rules contribute to this task by assigning to each daughter, other than verbs and conjunctions, a 'degree of peripherality' relative to all its sisters. In other words, it establishes a hierarchical order among the daughters, from 'least peripheral' to 'most peripheral'. This ordering is made use of by the sequence rules (S.8 and S.9), which basically put the daughters in order of peripherality, with the least peripheral first.

I have taken the notion (and the term) of peripherality from a paper by Alick Henrici (Huddleston et al. 1968, chap. 16) on the order of adverbials in a large sample of scientific English, in which he showed that, for example, adverbials of time, place and direction could be put into a hierarchical order according to which was most likely to be nearest the edge of the clause and which nearest its center (the verb), with time more peripheral than place and place more peripheral than direction. In other words, if a clause contains two of these adverbials, and both are at the end of the clause, then it is more likely that a place adverbial will follow a direction adverbial than the other way around, and so on. It is natural to extend the notion to include not only adverbials but also complements (including the subject), and this is how I am using it here. It will be seen from what follows that the use of the peripherality hierarchy is similar, in principle, to that of Jackendoff's 'thematic hierarchy' (1972: 43), although the latter is restricted only to complements and isn't used to predict sequence of elements. (It is also similar to the hierarchies of Perlmutter and Postal, and of Keenan, both discussed by Pullum—1975—who argues that in all languages the subject normally precedes the object, with a rather easily explicable exception.)

As Henrici shows in his study of adverbials, the relative peripherality of two adverbials depends on several different factors, which can conflict with each other. The two which he isolates are (*a*) the semantic type, such as 'place', 'time' and so on, (*b*) the syntactic type, such as clause, prepositional phrase and adverbial phrase. (He leaves open the possibility that the latter distinctions are simply a rough correlate of length, say in terms of number of words, and that it is really length which is the determining factor.) As one would except, clauses are more peripheral than prepositional phrases, and prepositional phrases are more peripheral than adverbial phrases. Similarly with complements: their position relative to other complements depends on a number of different factors, of which the 'semantic types' to which Jackendoff's hierarchy refers (agent, location, source, goal, theme) are only one. Others are (I surmise) (*b*) syntactic type —noun-phrases are less peripheral than prepositional phrases, nonclauses are less peripheral than clauses, pronouns are less peripheral than nonpronominal noun-phrases, (*c*) length— shorter items are less peripheral than longer ones, (*d*) prominence—less prominent items (as shown by intonation) are less peripheral than more prominent ones.

The interaction of these factors explains many facts about the order of elements which are hard to take account of in a transformational grammar. For example, if two elements following the verb would normally occur in the order A–B, the order may be B–A if A is much longer or more prominent than B (cf. *'he drives dangerously his car' but 'He drives dangerously every car that he hires from rent-a-car companies that are fool enough to accept him as a customer') and in some cases an order A–B which would normally be permitted is bad if B is 'lighter' than A (cf. 'John gave the man with red hair the books that he asked for', but ?'John gave the man with red hair the books' and *'John gave the man with red hair them'). Facts like this are hard to reflect in a grammar in the way other kinds of fact are reflected, because notions such as length and prominence are quantitative rather than qualitative, so it seems appropriate to use a different kind of apparatus to reflect them.

Like Jackendoff's thematic hierarchy, the peripherality hierarchy is regrettably undeveloped. It is clearly not enough to simply list the factors involved, as we did above—in writing a generative grammar you also have to spell out precisely how the factors interact with each other, which means saying which take priority over which—for example, the 'syntactic type' takes priority over the 'semantic type' in that, when the goal is a noun-phrase and the actor is a prepositional phrase, the latter is more peripheral than the former, although it is the less peripheral if both are noun-phrases. This explains the difference between active and passive sentences, the goal [+ nominal$^\leftarrow$ + transitive] (in terms of the rather crude analysis in our grammar) being a noun-phrase in both cases, but the actor being a noun-phrase in an active clause [+ nominal$^\leftarrow$ + predicate] and a prepositional phrase in a passive one [+ preposition$^\leftarrow$ + passive] (see sister-dependency rules SD.1, 2 and 3). On the other hand, semantic type takes priority over 'weight' in that the actor will be less peripheral than the goal, and the goal ('direct object') less peripheral than the beneficiary ('indirect object') come what may, provided they are both noun-phrases (cf. *'John gave the book some people who happened to be passing', *'The book wrote a linguist who doesn't believe in transformations'). It may be that the factors listed above play a part in determining peripherality in all languages, and maybe even different languages might be similar in the details of the factors (though the order of time and place adverbials notoriously differs in English and German); but I take it that the balancing of the factors against one another is something which can vary considerably from language to language. Since so much remains to be done before 'peripherality' can be called a well-defined concept, I have deliberately not tried to include any kind of peripherality-assignment rules in the grammar in Appendix 1.

How then would peripherality-assignment rules work, if we had any? For any clause, it would be possible to take all the daughters it is known to have, and compare them for peripherality. Unlike all the other types of rule, these wouldn't actually affect the structure directly at all, by requiring features (or functions) to be present, or requiring the elements that are present to be in a particular order; they would simply serve as aids in the application of other rules, in allowing one to identify, say, the least peripheral nominal in the clause if a rule referred to such a nominal.

It is perhaps important to explain that the sequence rules are not the only rules which refer to notions of peripherality—if they had been, there would have been no point in setting up such a troublesome type of rule rather than specifying relative sequence directly in terms of semantic types, syntactic types and so on. To the extent that peripherality controls a whole range of different types of rule, it clearly has some independent validity. The following are some other areas of syntax to which peripherality seems relevant. First, there is subject selection (see the function-assignment rule FU.2): the function SUBJECT is assigned to 'the least peripheral nominal complement of the verb(s)'. This automatically explains the difference in subject selection between active and passive clauses, as we have already seen. Moreover, it explains why *'This plate has never been eaten porridge from' is not possible, although 'This plate has never been eaten from' is: *this plate* is the least peripheral nominal in the second sentence, but not in the first (in which the least peripheral nominal is *porridge*). (For discussion of the difficulty of stating such restrictions in standard 'systemic' grammar, see Downes 1974.)

Second, there is 'topic' selection (function-assignment rule FU.7), which allows a complement other than the subject to be 'topicalized' only provided it is the *most* peripheral of the nominal complements. This predicts that *'The other girl John gave a different present' won't be grammatical, because *the other girl* is 'indirect object' and therefore has to be counted as less peripheral than *a different present*—hence the ungrammaticality also of *'John gave a different present the other girl'. The relative peripherality of direct objects compared with indirect objects (when both are nominals rather than prepositional phrases) is categorical (except for pronouns), in that relative length can't override it: *'John gave a present the girl he'd been courting for nine years' is just as bad as the second example above. In contrast with this, we find that length can override the rule that prepositional phrases (and their complements) are more peripheral than nominals: so 'John gave to Mary an enormous bunch of roses that he'd been growing secretly in his window box' is well-formed. Since the peripherality relation of nominals vis-à-vis prepositional phrases is less rigid, we should expect to find more latitude in the possibilities of topicalization, and this is precisely what we do find (though in this case length seems to play no part): alongside 'John gave a different present to the other girl' we find 'The other girl John gave a different present to', but we also find 'The other present John gave to a different girl', with *the other present* counting as more peripheral than *(to) a different girl*. (I owe this example to Paul Schachter.)

Turning to a different kind of 'topicalization', *'Who did John give a present?' is ruled out because *who* is topic but less peripheral than *a present*. Moreover, the topic in a wh-question is the wh-item itself, and the restriction this time is that the wh-item must be the *least* peripheral one in the clause, given that there may be others in a wh-question: 'Who said what?' but not *'What did who say?' (except as an echo-question, which isn't subject to this constraint); cf. also 'What did he give to whom?' but not *'To whom did he give what?' or *'Who did he give what to?'.

Third, the rule for front-shifting adverbials is sensitive to peripherality, as Henrici's figures show, in that the more peripheral an adverbial is, the more likely it is to be front-shifted. Moreover —and this may be connected—the more peripheral it is, the more chance it has of having a domain extending over several conjoined clauses (in other words, the more chance it has of being deleted by conjunction-reduction).

Finally, it seems that peripherality will be referred to in the treatment of pronominalization—which, of course, I assume to be a matter of semantic interpretation, with Jackendoff (1972), rather than of noun-phrases being converted into pronouns in the presence of a coreferential noun-phrase. The rules which relate the syntactic structure to a semantic structure showing coreference will have to be able to say something like this: if there is a pronoun P, and a noun-phrase N which is semantically able to refer to the same entity as P, and if P and N are clause-mates, then P and N may be coreferential only if P is more peripheral than N. This usually boils down to the same thing as saying that P must follow N, but if P is inside a topicalized complement it is P which comes first, so the relevant relation is peripherality rather than sequence. This explains why, in 'John's friends he would never abandon', it isn't possible for *John* and *he* to be coreferential, although it is possible in both 'John's friends will never abandon him' and 'His friends John will never abandon' (cf. Stockwell, Schachter and Partee 1973, chap. 5, section 2D).

Although this section has been concerned exclusively with peripherality in the clause, it seems likely that it would apply in other areas of syntax as well. One thinks in particular of the order of adjectives inside the noun-phrase, where a number of different factors seem to interact to determine order in much the same way that different factors interacted in determining order in the clause.

3.6. Function-assignment Rules

Like peripherality-assignment rules, function-assignment rules supply information about constituents which can be used by other rules, notably sequence rules, and isn't easily accessible in the form of features. However, unlike peripherality-assignment rules, function-assignment rules are responsible for the presence of specific labels in the structure. These labels represent functions, and to keep them distinct from feature labels, we write them in uppercase letters. We shall be concerned in this section (and for that matter in the grammar in Appendix 1) with only four functions: SUBJECT, TOPIC, SCENE-SETTER and RELATOR.

In standard transformational grammar, functional notions like 'subject' are not represented by means of labels (like 'SUBJECT'), but by means of configurations of category-symbols—the subject, for instance, is the NP which is immediately dominated by S, and the object is the one which is immediately dominated by VP (Chomsky 1965: 68). The same is true in principle of daughter-dependency grammar, since 'functional' definitions can be given by specifying dependency relations, as I explained in 3.1 —for instance, the equivalent of the transformational underlying object is defined as [+ Nominal ← + transitive], meaning 'the nominal which depends as a sister on the feature [+ transitive] of the verb'. At one time, indeed, I believed that there was no more need for functional labels in daughter-dependency (at that time 'systemic') grammar than there is claimed to be in transformational grammar (Hudson 1974), having previously believed, with other systemic linguists, that functional labels should be attached in bundles to every node in the structure (except the top one)—Hudson (1971). It now seems, however, that both these positions were wrong. There is a need for a very limited number of functional categories, which will be assigned only to a small number of nodes in the structure, namely, those right at the beginning of the clause. The reason is, as we have already suggested, that there are rules that need to refer to groupings of element which can't be defined in terms of features, as is normally possible. Let us consider some examples.

First, take the relation between wh-items in wh-questions and front-shifted adverbials. If the wh-question is a main clause, an adverbial can be moved up to the front, before the wh-item; but if it is an embedded clause, this isn't possible:

In France what kind of wine do they drink with fish?
*(I wonder) in France what kind of wine they drink with fish?

Why is this? It clearly has something to do with the fact that adverbials can't be moved forward in front of a relative pronoun either:

*(This is the kind of wine) in France which they drink.

On the other hand, it isn't a general ban on adverbial-fronting in embedded clauses, pace Emonds (1972) and the 'structure-preserving constraint', as witness this:

(I'm sure) that in France they don't drink wine like this
with fish.

But nor is it a ban which applies to embedded clauses other than those introduced by *that,* since the adverbial can't be moved into a position before *that,* unless it is moved right up to the beginning of the main clause:

*(I'm sure) in France that they don't drink wine like this
with fish.
In France (I'm sure) that they don't drink wine like this
with fish.

Clearly, the rule for embedded clauses is that the adverbial mustn't be put immediately before the item that 'introduces' the clause, whether this is *that* or a relative pronoun or a wh-item. Now the question is whether it is possible to formulate this restriction in terms of the features of the items concerned.

Assuming that 'adverbial' can be defined in terms of features, we can concentrate on the other set of items and ask whether they can be so defined. The answer is that they can't. For one thing, there is no other reason for giving different features to a wh-item according to whether the clause it introduces is embedded or not, since precisely the same range of items is possible in both kinds of clause. Consequently, the rule which prevented adverbial-fronting in embedded clauses would automatically prevent it in main clauses too—something we don't want, of course. And for another, the list of items covered by the putative set of features to which the rule would have to refer is too heterogeneous to be treated as a natural class. This becomes particularly clear when we consider that it includes finite auxiliary verbs like *had* and *should,* when these are used in a clause meaning *if* . . . : as far as the restriction on adverbial-fronting is concerned, such auxiliaries are just like ordinary conjunctions, although auxiliaries in main clauses allow adverbial-fronting:

> Last night had they arrived on time?
> *Last night had they arrived on time we shouldn't be in this mess now.

It seems, then, that the class of items which aren't allowed to have an adverbial fronted before them can't be defined in terms of features—in the one case because there are no feature differences between items that are relevant and others that aren't, and in the other case because the class would have to be defined by a disjunction of features, which we have ruled out a priori as explained in 2.2. This being so, we need to have some other cover-term for the class concerned, and for this we use the function-term RELATOR. As we shall see below, this term will be used in other rules too, so we haven't brought it in just in order to 'save' the adverbial-fronting rule from referring to a disjunction of features.

Now let us consider another example, involving the relation between wh-items and topicalized complements. The relevant facts are shown by the following paradigm:

> He bought the other one for somebody else.
> The other one he bought for somebody else.
> For whom did he buy the other one?
> *The other one for whom did he buy?

What is there about topicalized complements (*the other one*) and wh-items in wh-questions (*for whom*) which allows either of them to occur on its own at the front of the clause, but doesn't allow both of them to occur there? Answer: they both have the function TOPIC, and this function, like the others, can occur only once per clause. Therefore either of them can have it, on its own, but they can't both have it. This again is a rule which can't be formulated in terms of features, since the features of either wh-items or complements are the same whether they occur at the head of the sentence or not; moreover, there is no way of preventing more than one item from having the relevant features per clause—this could be done only by ruling out well-formed sentences like 'For whom did he buy the other one?' as well. (As Paul Schachter has pointed out to me, the term 'FOCUS' might have been better than 'TOPIC', because of the meanings of wh-items; unfortunately the suggestion reached me too late for me to change the terminology in the rest of the book.)

It will be seen that both of these first two arguments for including functional labels apply equally to transformational grammar and to daughter-dependency grammar: it is no easier to formulate the rules that we have been considering in transformational grammar than it would be in daughter-dependency grammar without functions. For example, wh-items and complements are each moved to the head of the clause by a separate transformation (question-formation and topicalization respectively), and have nothing in common there which would distinguish them from fronted adverbials, which it will be noticed are *not* subject to this constraint:

In France what kind of wine do they drink with fish?

Moreover, the possibility of a fronted adverbial before a fronted wh-item, as in this example, or of a *that* complementizer before a fronted complementizer ('I'm sure that wine like this they'd never drink with fish in France') rules out the two obvious possible solutions: treating both fronted wh-items and fronted complements as replacements for the element complementizer, as in Chomsky's proposals for wh-items (1973: 237), or simply 'Chomsky-adjoining' both of them to the rest of the clause containing them.

Another problem connected with fronted wh-items, which the use of function-labels solves, is that there may be no difference in actual position between a wh-item that has been fronted and one that hasn't. This is the case if the wh-item is subject, since it is already at the head of the sentence as subject. In spite of this lack of surface-markers, it is important to allow two different syntactic analyses for clauses like 'Who came late?', one with the wh-item fronted and the other with it unfronted. This is necessary for two reasons. First, it is semantically ambiguous between an 'ordinary question' interpretation and an 'echo-question' interpretation, the first being parallel to a clause like 'Who did you see?' and the second parallel to one like 'You saw who?'. By far the easiest way of relating the semantics to the syntax at this point is to allow the 'ordinary question' interpretation only when the wh-item has been fronted—which means allowing it to be treated as fronted even in 'Who came late?', where there is no sign of its having been fronted. Second, a complement can be topicalized if the wh-item is subject: 'The other cake who chose?'; but if there is a topicalized complement the only interpretation is the 'echo-question' one, as we would predict from the above, since topicalizing a complement should be possible only if the wh-item hasn't been fronted (if it has been, then there will be two items competing for the function TOPIC), and if it hasn't been fronted, the only interpretation possible should be the echo-question one. The use of functions allows us to show exactly the right relations: 'Who came late?' is ambiguous as to whether *who* is TOPIC, like *who* in 'Who did you see?', or not, like the *who* in 'You saw who?'. Without functions, the only possibility is some kind of change in dependency relations, as in the transformational analysis which treats *who* as a daughter of the clause if it's not fronted, but as a sister of the clause if it is; but as we have just seen this analysis has problems in accommodating adverbials that are preposed.

Still on the treatment of wh-items in questions, another advantage of using functions is that the rules which assign functions make many other rules unnecessary. As far as wh-items are concerned, the function-assignment rule for TOPIC (FU.6) does the work of the question-formation transformation, since it optionally allows TOPIC to be assigned to any wh-item in an interrogative clause (but not in any other kind of clause). Once TOPIC has been assigned to a wh-item, its position at the head of the clause is guaranteed, since there is a sequence rule (S.7) which puts all items with functions there, and another (S.6) which puts TOPIC before SUBJECT, if they are separate. Similarly, the function-assignment rule for TOPIC does duty for the topicalization transformation, as we have already shown, and the function-assignment rule for RELATOR replaces the rule for moving relative pronouns forward (if this rule is separate from the one for wh-items in clauses). Moreover, we can introduce a fourth function, called SCENE-SETTER (for lack of a better term), to be the function of a fronted adverbial, and the function-assignment rule for SCENE-SETTER (which isn't included in the grammar in Appendix 1) would then take over the job of the adverb-preposing transformation. In short, all transformations which move items to the left within the clause are replaced by function-assignment rules.

One advantage of replacing left-moving transformations by function-assignment rules is that it provides a formal explanation for the fact that such rules are 'unbounded'—they can move elements into the structure of a clause any distance up the tree. We shall return to this question in the discussion of 'raising', in 3.8, but we can explain briefly how raising is related to functions. A function-assignment rule both introduces a function as 'daughter' of some clause and assigns it to some item within the clause, the item being defined by a disjunction of features, as we shall see below. However, although the function itself has to be a daughter of the clause in whose structure the rule is applied, the item to which it is assigned need not be, but may be a grand-daughter or even more distantly related, though it must be a 'descendant'. (This is true, to be precise, of all the functions except SUBJECT.) In other words, the function-assignment rule for SCENE-SETTER, for example, can find its adverbial in any clause within the clause to which the function is attached as a daughter, thus allowing for examples like 'Tomorrow evening I think I may have promised Mary when I saw her last to go to the pictures with her'. (The rules will need to be restricted somehow to prevent them from 'looking' in relative clauses and adverbial clauses, but the restrictions seem to be the same for all the functions, so they could be stated as general restrictions on function-assignment rules.) The advantage that I am claiming for the daughter-dependency approach, then, is that it restricts 'unboundedness' to a general type of rule with many other formal idiosyncrasies, whereas in transformational grammar it is a property of a subset of transformations which are otherwise unified only by virtue of the fact that they move leftward within the clause (and even then some rules like the passive rule would have to be excluded).

Another, rather similar, advantage of the daughter-dependency approach is that it restricts the equivalent of deletion transformations to apply only to items that would have functions if they were there. This is the subject of section 3.9, so again all we need do here is mention it as a characteristic of functions. We shall see there that the rule for SUBJECT (and probably only for this one function, in fact) is formulated in such a way that there will be no subject in contexts where none is wanted—certain types of embedded nonfinite clauses, for instance. I shall also argue there that all the other phenomena that require deletion transformations in a transformational grammar can be handled in other ways in a daughter-dependency grammar, so it is possible to say that the only cases in which an element is 'suppressed' (in the terminology we shall use) involve functions, and maybe specifically the function SUBJECT.

Before turning to the formal properties of function-assignment rules, let us just note two other possible uses of functions, to explain some rather odd facts about English. First, it is well known, since Ross pointed it out (1967: 57), that sentences must not be 'clause-internal'—sentences must be either right at the beginning or right at the end of their main clause, but can't be in the middle. For example, they can't follow the auxiliary verb even when, as subjects, they ought to be able to:

*Did that John was late surprise you?

This restriction also applies to topicalized objects before a subject clause, although otherwise the objects ought to be able to be topicalized:

Anybody else the news about the accident would have
    shocked—but not John.

*Anybody else that Mary had died would have shocked—
     but not John.

This of course is ruled out by Ross's constraint (provided that a topicalized object isn't Chomsky-adjoined to the sentence out of which it is moved, as Ross's analysis of wh-movement requires wh-items to be—see above). But what Ross's constraint doesn't explain is why adverbials *may* be preposed before a subject clause:

After his recent behavior, that John was expelled will
     surprise nobody.

A possible explanation in functional terms would be that the only function that clauses like these can have in their own right is TOPIC—which immediately explains why a topicalized object isn't possible, although a fronted adverbial is, and will also explain why the auxiliary can't precede the clause, as we shall see below. On the other hand, it might be possible to formulate the rule for SUBJECT-assignment in such a way that a TOPIC clause could optionally be assigned SUBJECT as well as TOPIC (bundles of functions being normal as the rules are formulated at present), so that whenever a clause occurred as SUBJECT, it would have to be TOPIC as well. In this analysis, the only kind of item which could be SUBJECT without being TOPIC as well would be noun-phrases—but this class includes gerund-clauses, as we have seen (2.3), and gerund-clauses *can* be 'clause-internal', contrary to Ross's predictions (as pointed out by Satyanarayana 1973). The analysis would thus solve another of Ross's problems at the same time.

The last set of phenomena which we shall consider is illustrated by the ungrammaticality of *'Anything else would you like?'—a sentence in which the subject and verb are inverted and there is also a TOPIC (*anything else*). Why should this sentence be excluded, given the acceptability of the following?

Anything else you'd like—but not that.
Would you like anything else?

An analysis worth investigating would treat the auxiliary verb as TOPIC, just as we suggested treating the auxiliary *had* in 'had I known that' (= 'if I had known that') as RELATOR. This would automatically rule out another TOPIC such as *anyone else* in the examples above, and would simultaneously explain why the auxiliary preceded the SUBJECT—it does so for just the same reason that any TOPIC does. (Similarly, Halliday—1967: 213—suggests treating the inverted auxiliary as 'theme', his equivalent of my TOPIC.) One disadvantage of this analysis would be that it would obscure the similarity between wh-questions and yes-no questions, since the inverted auxiliary couldn't be TOPIC in wh-questions, where, as we have seen, the wh-item is TOPIC. Another is that it makes little sense semantically.

Let us now turn to the technical question of how functions are introduced (in other words, how we show in which clauses they occur and in which they don't) and how they are assigned to features, when they *are* present in a clause. The principle seems fairly clear: one set of rules introduce whichever functions are allowed or required, and another set assign them. The first set act like daughter-dependency rules, in that they take features of the clause and introduce functions as daughters of the clause, leaving a line between them to show the dependency (hence the line between clause and subject in the diagrams we have given as illustrations in some of the earlier sections). The second set define the features with which each function can combine, allowing a range of alternatives for each function (which is why functions are needed—in order to bring together a disjunction of feature-sets, as we showed earlier in this section). For examples the reader is referred to section J of Appendix 1, where the rules are arranged by function rather than by type.

The main problems are raised by the rules for introducing functions, since in some cases (notably that of RELATOR—see rule FU.10) the constraint is simply that it is introduced if there is a feature for it to be assigned to, and not otherwise. This raises the question of whether it is right to separate the introduction of functions from their assignment to features. Another problem is in deciding whether the functions TOPIC and SCENE-SETTER should be obligatory or optional. If they are obligatory, they can be allowed to combine with SUBJECT, or to remain separate from it; so in principle every clause would have a SCENE-SETTER and a TOPIC, but these wouldn't always be separate from each other or from the SUBJECT. Or should TOPIC and SCENE-SETTER be optional, occurring in some clauses but not in others? Clearly we need to allow TOPIC at least to combine with SUBJECT, for the sake of some of the types of sentence we have discussed in this section—for instance, wh-questions with the wh-item as subject, and clauses with embedded clauses as subject. However, it seems that at least some clauses *can't* have a TOPIC—such as some kinds of clauses with nonfinite verb (Langacker 1974)—and our analysis of wh-questions depended on there being no TOPIC in 'Who said it?' in one of its interpretations. Accordingly it looks as though we shall have to prevent TOPIC from occurring at all in some kinds of clause, and make it optional in other types. (Much the same will be true of SCENE-SETTER, I assume.) Then the problem arises as to how we decide whether a clause like 'The little dog laughed' has *no* TOPIC, or has a TOPIC combined with SUBJECT—both analyses being possible according to the above, although the sentence isn't at all ambiguous in meaning.

With regret I leave these problems unsolved, in the hope that some new facts will turn up to help solve them. To conclude this section, I shall point out that it may be necessary to postulate functions in the structure of the noun-phrase as well as in that of the clause, with which the discussion so far has been exclusively concerned. I have in mind, in particular, the first three or four places in a noun-phrase like 'all the other three boys', which show a pattern of relations remarkably similar to that which we find at the start of the clause. Notably, the features which are separated into a number of bundles in this example can be piled up into a single bundle (e.g. on 'another') just as the functions we have been discussing in the clause structure can be either separate or combined. On the other hand, it also seems that the relevant rules for noun-phrase structure can all be stated in terms of features, so it may be that we don't need functions there after all.

3.7. Sequence Rules

Having explained about peripherality and functions, we can now show how sequence rules work. It will be noticed that they are formulated in such a way that it is never necessary to *change* the order of elements—this would involve a distinction between underlying and surface structure such as is found in transformational grammar. Instead, the sequence that is defined by these rules is the sequence found in surface structure. As we shall explain below, many of the cases which in transformational grammars are handled by means of movement transformations are dealt with here by the ordering of sequence rules, but this ordering is of a very different kind from that found among transformations.

Sequence rules define the possible orders of daughters within one mother—they can't define the order of one element with reference to an element which isn't a sister of it. It is possible in this kind of grammar to make such a severe restriction on the scope of sequence rules because there is so little structure, compared with transformational grammar—that is, there are so few steps between the top of a structure diagram and its bottom; for instance, the clause is analyzed as 'subject + verb + object', rather than as 'subject + predicate/verb-phrase'. Had we had to have a verb-phrase for other reasons, it might have been necessary to change the character of sequence rules completely, since the verb would not have been a sister of the subject, but its niece, and it might have been necessary to refer to the ordering of subject and verb. As it is, this problem doesn't arise, and all sequence rules can be understood to apply just to sisters.

There are several different types of sequence rule, as a glance at section K of the grammar in Appendix 1 will show. For instance, some are such that they can easily be formalized by a formula in which two elements are defined and an arrow is put between them, showing that they have to occur in the order in which they appear in the formula; and others are such that they have to take the form of a statement in ordinary language. Moreover, they vary in the kinds of factor they take account of, according to whether they refer to features or functions or peripherality or dependency or a mixture, and according to whether they refer to *specific* features or functions, or to general properties such as having a function of any kind. To bring some kind of order into the list of sequence rules, they have been divided into four main types:

- (*a*) those that refer to specific features;
- (*b*) those that refer to functions but not to specific features;
- (*c*) those that refer to peripherality;
- (*d*) those that refer to dependency.

This division does not seem entirely arbitrary, but reflects what I believe to be a distinction among four rather different factors which combine to determine the order of elements in syntax. For instance, I should predict that languages would be most similar in their dependency-based rules and least similar in their feature-based rules. Moreover, as we have already seen, the four different kinds of property of items on which the distinction is based are very different from one another. I therefore make no apology for the fact that there are such different types of sequence rule; rather, I believe that this variation reflects a genuine property of language, which, be it noted, is *not* reflected in transformational grammars.

We can now look briefly at the four types of rule in turn.

(*a*) *Feature-based rules.* It will be seen from section K of Appendix 1 that there are two kinds of feature-based rule: one which locates one item in front of another, and one which identifies one item with another. The first type is written 'A $\Rightarrow$ B', where at least one of A and B is a set of features, and the big-headed arrow means 'precedes'. (Notice that, unlike the small-headed dependency arrows, this one does *not* get put into the structure diagram.) The simplest example of this type of rule is S.5, '[+ article] $\Rightarrow$ [− article]', which makes sure that if a noun-phrase contains an article and a noun they must come in that order. The second type of rule is written 'A = B', where both A and B must be features. The only example of this type of rule is S.3, '[+ finite] = [+ finite]'. This says, 'If a clause is such that it ought to contain two finite verbs, it will in fact only contain one, which will satisfy both the dependency rules concerned'. This rule is needed because there are two sources for finite verbs, but no clause in fact contains more than one. On the one hand, there is the daughter-dependency rule which introduces a 'predicate' element into every clause (DD.1), together with the feature-addition rule FA.7 which says that normally this predicate element will be a finite verb. On the other hand, there is another daughter-dependency rule which says that a non-embedded interrogative clause should contain a finite verb (this is DD.2). (The reason for having this second source for finite verbs is that some non-embedded interrogatives are [+ optative], i.e. 'imperatives', and such clauses have no other reason for containing a finite verb—indeed, their 'predicate' element is required by FA.6 to be an infinitive; examples are 'Shall I open the window?' and 'Why don't you be quiet?!'.) Therefore, when the conditions are satisfied for *both* rules to apply, we have to prevent the clause from containing two separate finite verbs, and this is done by rule S.3.

It wouldn't be at all surprising if one found another language that contained neither of the two rules that we have just discussed—indeed, there *are* languages that have neither (languages that have articles after nouns or that don't allow interrogative imperatives of the type we have in English). The same is true of all the other feature-based rules in Appendix 1. Rule S.1 inverts the subject and first auxiliary in an interrogative clause; most languages don't do this. S.2 makes sure that S.1 doesn't invert the subject with the main verb; German allows this to happen, and therefore obviously lacks this rule. S.4. keeps clauses with (interrogative) *if* or zero as 'complementizer' after the verb of the matrix clause; presumably French lacks this rule, since it lacks the distinction *if/whether* and *that/∅*. Feature-based rules are clearly as language-specific as rules can be.

(*b*) *Function-based rules.* There are only two function-based rules—which is already a big difference compared with feature-based rules. The first orders the four functions relative to one another, using the sign '⇒' (an equal sign combined with a large-headed arrow) to show that the left-hand function either precedes or is combined with the right-hand one. Since any logically possible combination of functions has to be allowed for, all the functions have to be ordered at the same time, by the same rule—whereas feature-based rules order elements in pairs only. It is this rule which puts the TOPIC before the SUBJECT and after the RELATOR when they are all separate, as in:

(I'm sure) that   this kind of wine   they   wouldn't drink.
       RELATOR   TOPIC   SUBJECT

It also combines them, however, on a single node, as in:

(I'm not sure) what kind of wine   is best with fish.
                RELATOR
                TOPIC
                SUBJECT

The second function-based rule simply puts all items with functions in front of those without functions—reflecting the fact that functions are responsible for the left-hand end of the clause.

How universal these rules are it's hard to know, but at least some variation is likely, since for one thing some languages presumably don't have RELATOR (i.e. they don't have 'complementizers', relative pronouns and the like), and languages with VSO order, or free order, will presumably make quite different arrangements. On the other hand, one might expect a fair degree of similarity among languages in their function-based rules.

(*c*) *Peripherality-based rules*. The first of the peripherality-based rules looks a good candidate for universality, since it says simply 'Less peripheral precedes more peripheral'; assuming that subjects are always less peripheral than objects, this explains why languages in which subjects precede objects (irrespective of the place of the verb) are so overwhelmingly more common than those with the object first.

The other two peripherality-based rules look rather more language-specific, though it would certainly be surprising to find a language with these rules reversed, say. The first one (S.9) tells how to cope with the following situation: according to the analysis for which I shall argue in chapter 4, a clause can contain two verbs, each of which allows one or more nominal complements, but one pair of complements (one from each verb) must be merged into a single nominal. The question is, *which* pair; and the answer is, the most peripheral complement of the first verb and the least peripheral one of the second (i.e. the dependent verb). Typical first verbs are *try* and *persuade;* each of them allows an infinitive to depend on it, and this infinitive will naturally allow a range of complements of its own. *Try* allows only one nominal complement (its subject), so this rule merges this complement with the least peripheral complement of the infinitive, i.e. with the infinitive's subject. This is how daughter-dependency grammar deals with the 'problem' of verbs like *try,* whose underlying subjects have to be the same as the underlying subject of their complement-clause—a relation which is virtually impossible to capture in a transformational grammar, as is well known. In a daughter-dependency grammar, rule S.9 simply makes sure that the [+ nominal] depending on *try* is the same *node* as the [+ nominal] depending on the infinitive. As for *persuade,* the same kind of restriction holds, except that this time the merged complements have to be the most peripheral of the two complements of *persuade* (i.e. its object) and the subject of the infinitive. The other peripherality-based rule does rather similar things for constructions in which a verb has a clause as a complement, and that clause has either a raised subject or complement as a sister (see 3.8), or an expletive *it* (see sister-dependency rule SD.16).

One might speculate that any language which has verbs like *try* and *persuade,* or which allows raising or extraposition (the two constructions covered by the second rule), will contain rules very much like these two, though there might be languages that didn't need them.

(*d*) *Dependency-based rules.* The only two dependency-based rules in our grammar are both extremely general. The first says that if one item A has a feature which depends, as a sister, on a feature of another item B, then A and B should be as close together as possible—and the dependent one (A) should follow.

This second part, about sequence, is very tentative, as we have already noted, so we may ignore it. The other part is obviously of very general applicability, and is a very natural rule for any language to have. It means, for instance, that there is no need to have a constituent containing prepositions and their complements, since the latter depend on the former (by sister-addition rule SD.17), and if there is no reason for splitting the two, they must naturally be next to each other; which means that 'stranded prepositions' (such as in 'What did he write with?') are not a source of discontinuity as such, but only a case where there is a reason for a dependent item to be separated from the item on which it depends. The other dependency-based rule is much more complex, and is needed mainly to keep grammars reasonably simple, by making it unnecessary to merge features explicitly in some cases where they need merging into a single bundle. For example, sister-dependency rule SD.4 says that if a verb has the feature [+ S-comp], it must have a clause as complement; and SD.5 says that if a verb has the feature [+ verbless-comp], which depends on [+ S-comp] in the classification rules, then it must have a verbless clause as complement. What the second dependency-based sequence rule does in cases like this is to say that the features introduced by the two dependency rules must be combined into one bundle—in this case, the verbless clause required by SD.5 is the same clause as the one required by SD.4. Once again, this rule is a very natural one for any grammar to contain and it wouldn't be at all surprising to find it in every language in the world.

This completes our survey of the four types of sequence rule, and it remains only to say something about the *ordering* relation among them—which, incidentally, will be seen to add further support for the distinction we have made. The fact is, as the reader will have noticed, that different rules can conflict with one another, and the grammar has to provide some way of resolving the conflict in favor of one of the conflicting rules—otherwise very many perfectly good sentences would be ruled out because they infringed some sequence rule. For example, rule S.1 says that the finite auxiliary may precede the subject, but rule S.7

says that all items with functions precede all those without functions—which means, according to the present analysis at least, that the subject (which has a function) should always precede the finite auxiliary (which doesn't have one). Therefore a sentence like 'Have you finished?' is ruled out by S.7, although it is formed according to S.1.

One way of solving this problem would be to expand the individual sequence rules by adding whatever exceptions and conditions were needed. A much more satisfactory solution, however, would be to give the rules a priority rating, saying which should take priority over which in cases of conflict—so S.1, for instance, would take priority over S.7. In other words, there would be a general convention that rules may be infringed provided this is required in order for a rule with a higher priority rating to be satisfied. Thus, as in transformational grammar, we have an *extrinsic* ordering of rules (Hudson 1974, McCord 1975)—but with two major differences. First, the effect of the ordering is just the reverse of that in transformational grammar, where the last rule is the one that has the last say, so to speak. In daughter-dependency grammar, on the contrary, the last word goes to the *first* rule—once it has spoken, no other rule is allowed to undo its effect. What this means is that in daughter-dependency rules the early rules are responsible for exceptional cases, and the late rules show what the normal sequence of elements is—whereas in transformational grammar, the first structure generated is meant to reflect the normal state of affairs, and deviations from this normal state are introduced by transformations. The second major difference from transformational grammar is that the extrinsic ordering in daughter-dependency grammar can apparently be imposed on *types* of rule, rather than on individual rules. In fact, it seems that the order of priority is:

(*a*) feature-based rules;
(*b*) function-based rules;
(*c*) peripherality-based rules;
(*d*) dependency-based rules.

Taking the same pair of rules again as an example, we see that the conflict between S.1 and S.7 will be resolved in favor of S.1, because this is a feature-based rule and S.7 is a function-based one. This ordering gives striking confirmation not only of the decision to distinguish these four particular types of rule, but also of the decision to make use of the concepts 'function', 'peripherality' and 'dependency'.

3.8. Raising and Discontinuity

We have now finished the discussion of the different types of structure-building rule found in a daughter-dependency grammar, and the remainder of the chapter will be devoted to showing how these rules between them cope with two of the main types of construction which are used as arguments for having transformations. In this section we shall discuss cases of so-called raising of one item into the structure of a higher clause, and the discontinuities that result from this; and in the next section we shall take up the question of how 'understood' elements are handled. In this section, then, we shall be showing how daughter-dependency grammar does without *movement* rules, and in the next how it does without *deletion* rules.

For convenience we shall divide the discussion in this section into three sections, each dealing with a different kind of 'raising', and therefore involving a different range of transformations:

    (*a*) topicalization, adverb-preposing, wh-movement;
    (*b*) tough-movement;
    (*c*) subject-raising.

It will be seen that the structures which we shall generate will all have the same property, of including items with two mothers; schematically, as in fig. 13.

C is the item which a transformational grammar would treat as 'raised', B the clause in which it started life, and A the clause in which it ended up. In this analysis, however, C is shown as a daughter of both A *and* B at the same time, with advantages that we have already discussed in connection with the concord rules for Greek participles (3.2 above). Given this analysis, the term

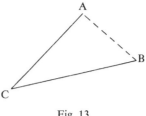

Fig. 13

'raising' isn't particularly appropriate—'lowering' would have been at least as good—but I shall continue to use the term for convenience.

(*a*) *Topicalization, adverb-preposing, wh-movement.* These three rules all have the property of raising an element unboundedly to the left, as we saw in our discussion of functions (3.6). (In this section I shall use the term 'wh-movement' to cover both the 'question-formation' transformation and the 'relative-clause–formation' one; it will make no difference to my claims if these are taken as two separate transformations.) For example, take the following sentence:

What do you think that John told her that he had arranged
    to do?

The raised item is *what,* since it belongs both to the main clause and to the clause whose verb is *do.* In transformational terms, the wh-movement rule moves *what* out of the clause containing *do,* up into the clause at the top. However one shows the facts about this sentence, they are reasonably clear: *what* acts as the wh-item which introduces the wh-question (coextensive with the whole sentence), but it also acts as the object of *do;* it is *not* object of the main clause, nor is the clause containing *do* a wh-question, or any other kind of interrogative for that matter. These facts have to be shown by any grammar.

The daughter-dependency treatment makes use of the function-assignment rules for TOPIC. This function is introduced as a daughter of the main clause (FU.5), and because the latter is [+ interrogative] the rule for assigning it (FU.6) is allowed to look around for a wh-item [+ wh-phrase] to assign it to. However, the rule specifically allows it to look among the 'constituents' (not just the *immediate* constituents) of the main clause for such an item, and so there is nothing to stop it from choosing the *what* which is object of *do* in the sentence above. The one restriction (which need not be stated explicitly in the rule) is that the item it chooses should be needed in the sentence for other reasons, and this is the case with *what,* which is in fact needed as object of *do.* The result is that the node representing *what* will be connected upward to the top node because of the daughter status of the function TOPIC, but it will also be connected sideways to the node representing *do,* because of its sister-dependency on the latter as object. Finally, a very general convention brings in the 'top-down priority' which is represented in transformational grammar by the cyclic ordering of rules: that the position of an item is always determined by the rules that apply to the highest structure to which it belongs—in this case, by the rules for positioning TOPIC. This being so, *what* is separated from the rest of the lower clause, which takes its normal position. Hence the *discontinuity* of *what . . . to do.*

It is worth pointing out here that the discontinuity of *what . . . to do* doesn't infringe the normal rules of sequence, provided we add another rule (FU.8) that assigns the function TOPIC to the raised item within its lower clause, in addition to the TOPIC which it has in the higher clause. By adding this general rule, we explain two things. First, why the lower clause can't have another TOPIC once one has been raised out of it in this way. We can see this by taking the following set of sentences:

He says that the other wine we should drink chilled.
How does he say that we should drink the other wine?
*How does he say that the other wine we should drink?

According to our analysis, the third sentence is bad because the embedded clause contains two TOPICs: *how* and *the other wine.* It is hard to see how this restriction could be reflected in a transformational grammar. Second, our analysis explains why it is that all raising in English is to the left: this is the only direction which wouldn't lead to an infringement of the sequence rules. Raising to the left is all right because all raising is done in terms of functions, and all functions are at the left; so if some function is moved further to the left, it'll still be in its right position relative to the rest of the elements in the lower clause. If raising were to the right, though, it would either move a function to the right of the rest of the lower clause, or be done without reference to functions at all.

For the record, there is one problem (of which I'm aware) with this analysis: it is possible for the 'complementizer' *that* to come after the TOPIC when the TOPIC is raised, although we have assumed that *that* is a RELATOR, and should therefore never follow TOPIC (rules S.6 and FU.10):

What do you think that she'll do?

On the other hand, as we would expect from our rules, *that* can't follow the SUBJECT of the embedded clause if this is raised (for an explanation see Hudson 1972, and for a refutation see Bresnan 1972):

*Who do you think that will come?

Clearly something is wrong with our analysis—possibly it is wrong to assume that *that* is RELATOR.

Similar analyses would be given to sentences like the following, in which the raised item isn't a wh-item:

The other books I think he said I should leave here.
Tomorrow evening I promised Mary that I'd take her out.

In these sentences the raising and discontinuity would be handled in just the same way as in the other cases we have been discussing, via the function-assignment rules for TOPIC (*the other books*) and SCENE-SETTER (*tomorrow evening*).

It may be helpful if we give here an example of the kind of structure which would be generated for a sentence like 'What do you think she did?' (see fig. 14).

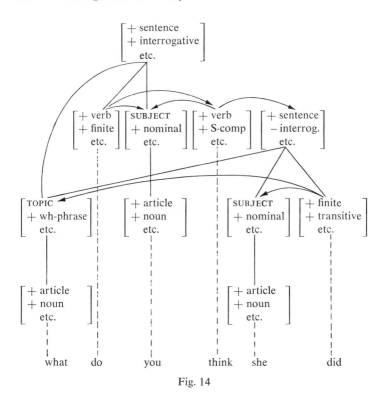

Fig. 14

(*b*) *Tough-movement.* The traditional transformational analyses of sentences like 'John is easy to please' treat *to please John*
as the subject of *is easy* in deep structure, and then move *John,*
by so-called 'tough-movement', into subject position instead of
the whole clause. Recently, an alternative analysis has become
popular, involving 'tough-deletion' rather than 'tough-movement': in deep structure *John* will be shown as both subject of
is easy and object of *please,* and will then be deleted from the
latter position. Of the two, the evidence seems to favor tough-
deletion (Lasnik and Fiengo 1974), but the issue is still very
much alive in transformational grammar. The analysis I shall
suggest manages to get the best of both worlds: it treats *John* as

subject of *is easy,* but it avoids deleting *John* from the embedded clause. It also explains some otherwise inexplicable facts.

As with the first kind of raising, this kind is handled in daughter-dependency grammar by means of functions; but unlike the other kind, this kind is governed—with some predicates (like *easy*) it is possible, but with others it isn't. To show this government we classify predicates, or more precisely adjectives (since no verbs allow it), as either allowing it or not. Those that do allow it have the feature [+ object-raising comp], and those that don't, don't (see rule C.26). We also classify infinitive clauses according to whether or not they have their object raised out of them (C.8), and we can then relate the two classifications by requiring that the sentential complement of a [+ object-raising comp] adjective should be a [+ object-raising] clause (by sister-dependency rule SD.8). The remaining problem, then, is making sure that the object of an [+ object-raising] clause is raised to act as subject of the [+ object-raising comp] adjective.

There are two aspects to the attack on this problem. On the one hand there is the rule for raising, and on the other the rules for assigning functions as appropriate to the raised item. The raising is done by a sister-dependency rule (SD.15) which also raises subjects, as we shall see in the next subsection. The rule says '+ raising→ + nominal', meaning 'If a clause is [+ raising] (whether the raised item is to be subject or object), it must have a nominal as its sister'. This nominal is, of course, the one which is raised, to act as a sister of the clause within which it is also a daughter. Having accounted for its sisterhood, the grammar then has to account for its daughterhood, and this is done by means of function-assignment rules: the rule for TOPIC assigns TOPIC to this nominal (FU.9), the TOPIC in question being the one that depends as a daughter on the [+ object-raising] clause itself. This shows the daughterhood of the raised object. The function-assignment rules also allow some complement of the verb in this clause to be assigned TOPIC (FU.6); and we make sure that the item selected will be object rather than subject by the rule (FU.1) for the presence of SUBJECT, which in fact prevents SUBJECT from being present in any [+ object-raising] clause. Finally, we have to show that the raised object is SUBJECT in the main clause; this is ensured by the fact that the raised nominal, qua sister of the [+ raising] clause, is the least peripheral nominal in the main clause, and therefore automatically qualifies as SUBJECT by FU.2. Fig. 15 shows the kind of structure that results. It will be seen that no place is allowed for *is:* this is because the complement of attributive *be* is treated as an embedded sentence, as we shall explain in 4.6. Consequently, to simplify the diagram I have left out the topmost clause, with *is* as its verb.

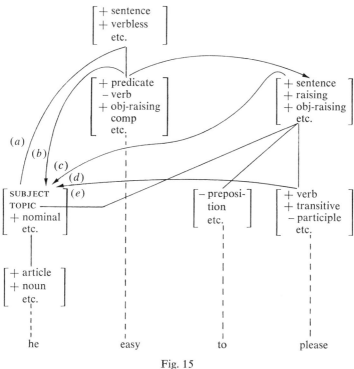

Fig. 15

It will be seen that no fewer than five dependency lines lead to the nominal (*he*), and for convenience I have labeled them (*a*) to (*e*). (*a*) connects it as daughter to the top clause (in the diagram), via the function SUBJECT (FU.1); (b) connects it as sister to the adjective *easy,* via the feature [+ nominal] (SD.1); (c) connects it as sister to the embedded clause, via [+ nominal] depending on [+ raising] (SD.15); (d) connects it as sister to the verb *please,* via [+ nominal] and [+ transitive] (SD.2); and (e) connects it as daughter to the embedded clause, via the function TOPIC and [+ obj-raising] (FU.5).

It is interesting to compare this analysis with one suggested recently by Chomsky (1973: 264), which also takes advantage (as this one does) of the fact that [+ object-raising] clauses can't have a subject of their own (Berman 1973). Chomsky suggests that the object should first be shifted into the (empty) subject position, by a special transformation, and then the old object can be deleted by the ordinary rules for deleting subjects, rather than by a special rule for deleting objects. There are a number of differences, all of which show our approach has an advantage over Chomsky's. To make it easier to refer to the elements concerned, we can take 'John is easy to please' as the example sentence throughout, except where we bring in other examples.

First, Chomsky says that *John* is subject of *to please* at some stage in the derivation, whereas I deny that *to please* has a subject at any stage, and claim that *John* is TOPIC, not SUBJECT. There are two reasons for claiming that *John* is TOPIC, and none for claiming that it's SUBJECT—indeed, as we shall see below, there is a reason for claiming it *isn't* SUBJECT. The first reason for claiming that it is TOPIC is that no other TOPIC is possible in the embedded clause once *John* has been treated in this way. Compare the following (in which it is assumed, reasonably I think, that *from this bank* is a complement of *borrow* and therefore has the function TOPIC rather than SCENE-SETTER when fronted):

From this bank it's hard to borrow money.
Money it's hard to borrow from this bank.
*From this bank money it's hard to borrow.

Money is hard to borrow from this bank.
*From this bank money is hard to borrow.

The reason for both of the starred sentences being ungrammatical is the same: in both cases the embedded clause would have to have two TOPICs, *from this bank* and *money*. Given that *from this bank* can be fronted in the first sentence, it is hard to see how any transformational analysis, including Chomsky's, could prevent it from being fronted in the other sentences as well. If we take *money* as TOPIC, however, we immediately predict exactly this pattern. (Notice, incidentally, that an adverbial *can* be fronted along with money: cf. 'Without a credit card money is hard to borrow'.)

Another argument in support of our analysis is that the item which is raised by tough-movement is subject to precisely the same constraints as those moved by wh-movement (Lasnik and Fiengo 1974: 550). In particular, an indirect object can be moved only if it has *to* with it:

John is easy to give advice to.
*John is easy to give advice.

These sentences can be compared with the following:

Who did you give advice to?
*Who did you give advice?

The explanation our grammar offers for this pattern is that *John* is TOPIC when it is raised in sentences like 'John is easy to please', but the rule for assigning TOPIC (FU.7) requires it to be the most peripheral complement—as it is if it has *to,* but not if it doesn't, when it is indirect object. (Lasnik and Fiengo offer no explanation.)

Another difference between our analysis and Chomsky's is that in his the rule which moves the object forward has to be sensitive to the features of the predicate in the next sentence up: if the latter is like *easy,* the movement can take place, otherwise it can't. In comparison with other transformational rules this is a very suspicious one, since one would normally expect movement entirely within the bounds of one clause to be governed by the predicate of that clause, rather than by the predicate of the next clause up (though the 'higher verb' analysis of questions would make subject-verb inversion and wh-movement sensitive to the presence of a predicate like *ask* in the next clause up). In our analysis, on the other hand, there is no need to establish a direct connection between *John* and *easy: easy* is related to the whole of the embedded clause, by a sister-dependency rule requiring the latter to be [+ object-raising], and then it is the feature [+ object-raising] that determines that *John* will be raised.

Finally, there is the old problem of having to specify in a transformational grammar that two separate NP nodes need to be identical, so that one of them can later be deleted. This is a problem with verbs like *try,* and it is also a problem with any analysis of sentences like 'John is easy to please' which have *John* in two places in deep structure (including Chomsky's). So far as I know there is no way in which a transformational grammar can formalize the constraint on deep structures that if the main predicate is *easy,* the subject of the main clause must be identical to the object of the embedded clause, short of imposing a 'deep-structure constraint' (Ross 1967, Perlmutter 1971) on structures which will filter out all the structures which don't meet the requirement —a different constraint, incidentally, being needed for *try,* for *persuade* and for *easy.* This amounts to a gesture of despair. In our analysis the problem doesn't arise: there is no sense in which there are two occurrences of *John* in the structure of 'John is easy to please', so there is no need to find a way to require identity of the two occurrences, as in Chomsky's analysis.

(*c*) *Subject-raising.* The last type of raising is meant to cover both 'subject-raising to subject position' (as in 'John seems to like Mary') and 'subject-raising to object position' (as in 'Everyone believes John to like Mary'). One of the advantages of the daughter-dependency approach is that it allows a unitary treatment of the two kinds of subject-raising, which is impossible in at least the standard transformational analysis, as has been shown for instance by McCawley (1970). I shall take it for granted that subjects *can* be raised to object position, although Chomsky has attempted to show that this isn't so. There seems little point in adding to the arguments that Postal uses (1974), but it is worth pointing out that Chomsky's alternative (1973) depends very heavily on the assumption that the type of clause which allows rules like reflexivization to cross its boundaries can be identified in terms of the nonfiniteness of its verb, in spite of the existence of nonfinite verbs in 'subjunctive' clauses, which don't allow such rules to cross their boundaries (cf. *'I recommend that myself be chosen').

The daughter-dependency analysis of subject-raising is rather like that of tough-movement, except that it is somewhat simpler. I assume, first, that subject-raising isn't governed by the main predicate as tough-movement was: what the predicate decides is whether it can take a clausal complement or not, and, if it can, whether the complement-clause will have a finite or a nonfinite verb. Main predicates are further classified (C.23) as [± epistemic], and whenever a predicate has [+ epistemic] and also the feature [– *that*-comp] which says it has a nonfinite complement, it can be assumed that its complement will have a raised subject. (It's not clear at present whether subject-raising occurs in non-epistemic environments—I shall assume it doesn't.) Thus once one knows that a verb like *seem* or *believe* is [+ epistemic] and [– *that*-comp], one knows first that it will have a clausal complement, second that the complement will have an infinitive as first verb, and third that the complement's subject will be raised. These facts are all formalized in the sister-dependency rule SD.7, which says that such a verb must have a complement with the features [+ nominal, – optative, – object-raising]. Now it will be recalled that the feature [± object-raising] presupposes [+ raising], which triggers the sister-dependency rule SD.15 which adds a nominal as sister to the clause; this is the rule which was responsible for the raising part of tough-movement. The function-assignment rule FU.3 says that this extra nominal must also be SUBJECT within the clause to which it is a sister, and this guarantees that it will be integrated into the structure of the embedded clause. It remains only to identify the raised nominal as subject or object in the main clause, and this is done very simply by the function-assignment rule for SUBJECT (FU.2) and the peripherality rules: if it is the least peripheral nominal, it will be assigned the function SUBJECT (and therefore automatically placed in front of the main predicate); otherwise it won't, and it will be left next to the complement-clause. The difference between *seem* and *believe* is that *seem* is [– transitive] and *believe* is [+ transitive], so by sister-dependency rule SD.2 *believe* will be accompanied by an extra nominal which will count as less peripheral than the raised one, and therefore prevent the latter from being made SUBJECT. (The raised nominal is combined with the most peripheral nominal complement by sequence rule S.10.)

After this condensed exposition of the daughter-dependency analysis, it may be helpful to have diagrams showing the structures generated for sentences containing *seem* and *believe* (see figs. 16 and 17).

3.9. Understood Elements

In this section I hope to show that daughter-dependency grammar doesn't suffer from the fact that it contains no rules for deleting items. It is clearly important to show this, since deletion rules are a kind of transformation, and the main theme of the book is that it is possible to write a grammar that contains no transformations but that is at least as good as a transformational grammar. If we can do without deletion rules it will be pure gain, since transformational theory is at present beset with problems raised only by the existence of such transformations: in particular, what is meant by two noun-phrases being 'identical', and are all deletions recoverable from the sentence to which they applied (as opposed to the general linguistic or extralinguistic context)? In arguing that deletions have no place in syntax, I shall of course be implying that 'understood' elements are to be identified in the semantics, which seems the right place for them to be. I have nothing useful to say about how this is to be done, but I take it that this is not a reason for keeping deletion rules in syntax.

Deletion transformations cover a wide range of syntactic phenomena, so we shall have to consider the different types of phenomena separately, showing for each one how it is handled in the daughter-dependency approach. We start with the easiest type, exemplified by *to*-deletion, complementizer-deletion, *it*-deletion,

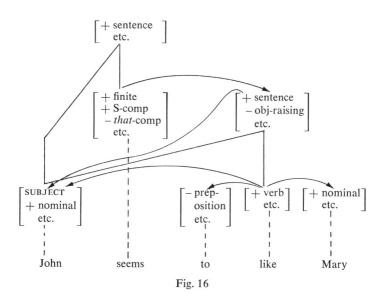

Fig. 16

Fig. 17

agent-deletion and (possibly) preposition-deletion. Instead of introducing the items concerned and then deleting them, we shall be able to avoid introducing them at all, except where they are allowed to remain in surface structure. For instance, in passive clauses the presence of the by-agent is optional (by SD.3), just like that of, say, an instrument adverbial (see the arguments in Sampson 1972); *it* is introduced optionally as a sister of an embedded clause (SD.16), but once it is in, it stays; and *to* will be introduced only where it is needed, by SD.14 (to be contrasted with SD.13).

The next type is 'whiz-deletion', alias relative-clause reduction. This is supposed to delete a relative pronoun plus *is,* converting, say, 'Who is sitting over there' into 'sitting over there'. This analysis faces insuperable problems in the form of sentences like 'Anyone finding a small black puppy will be rewarded', which does not come from 'anyone who is finding . . . ', and in sentences like 'The man sitting next to me got up', which would have to come from 'the man who *was* sitting . . . '. Moreover, 'All books published since 1900 are kept in that room' would have to come from 'all books which *have been* published . . . ' (see Hudson 1973 for further discussion). Instead of this problematic analysis, we simply generate reduced relative clauses directly, allowing them to have a participle as first verb (by rule FA.5).

Third, there is 'sluicing', the transformation which converts, say, 'He did something but I don't know what he did' into 'He did something but I don't know what' (Ross 1969*b*). On the assumption that deletions have to be recoverable, this rule won't be able to apply to main clauses, so a different way will have to be found for generating one-word questions like 'Why?', as main clauses—or, for that matter, in embedded clauses where the 'understood' material isn't present in the sentence. Rather than have two different sources for such clauses according to whether they are produced by deletion of recoverable material or not, I favor a single analysis in which such clauses are generated directly, without deletion. At present I can't offer details on how this is to be done, but the general approach seems fairly clear: allow the 'item' which is introduced as a dependent daughter of [+ sentence] to be any one of: *yes, no, so, not, why, how* and so on (allowing the wh-items to be accompanied optionally by *not*). The selection from this list will depend on the features of the clause —if the clause is [+ interrogative], it will have to be a wh-item (yes-no questions don't occur in this abbreviated form), but if [– interrogative], *yes, no* (if [– nominal]), *so, not* (if [+ nominal]).

The fourth type of deletion is comparative-deletion, which generates constructions like 'John is bigger than Bill' out of 'John is bigger than Bill is'. I see no reason at present not to analyze *than Bill* as a prepositional phrase, for the reasons given by Hankamer (1973). Even if a transformational grammar were to let *than Bill* start off, in deep structure, as a full clause and then end up as a prepositional phrase, it would have to have unusually powerful transformations en route to change a clause into a prepositional phrase. It will be objected that the prepositional analysis of *than* fails to capture the ambiguity of sentences like 'John likes Bill more than Peter', but to this it can be replied that the same problem arises with other prepositions, such as *before, like* and *with* or *without,* for which the underlying clause analysis is much less attractive; all the following sentences, for example, are ambiguous in the same way:

John saw Bill before Peter.
John treats Bill like Peter.
John attacked Bill with Peter.
John defeated Bill without Peter.

In other words, the ambiguity is a purely semantic one, which need not be reflected in the syntax, so the prepositional analysis is appropriate. There is then no special problem about *than* or *as,* since they both take nominal complements just like other prepositions. (It may be that adjectives and verbs can be complements of *than:* 'She is more pretty than beautiful', and so on; but even here ordinary prepositions are possible, as for instance *except* and *but:* 'She is everything except pretty', 'She is anything but pretty'.)

Fifth, we have 'VP-deletion'—the transformation which reduces full sentences like 'He was singing an old song' to *he was,* by deleting the verb-phrase. Once again we have the problem of recoverability, since the 'model' sentence needn't be in the same sentence; and the problem of identity, since sentences like 'Mary was cutting her toenails and John was too' are permitted, even where John is understood to cut his own toenails, not Mary's. In our grammar the reduced forms of sentences are easy to generate, simply by making the rules for introducing verbs as complements optional: as we shall see in the next chapter, the first verb is introduced by a daughter-dependency rule but all the following ones are introduced by a chain of sister-dependency rules (unless they are in an embedded clause, in which case the same principle still applies), so the chain can be stopped at any point, even if the only verb generated so far is the first one, an auxiliary. This analysis, incidentally, will also cover tag questions, except for explicitly allowing them to occur in a clause's structure, since tags are simply ordinary, reduced, yes-no interrogatives (as I have argued in Hudson 1975).

The sixth type of deletion rule purports to delete the subject of a nonfinite verb under specified conditions. Transformational grammars generally have two rules for this, one for imperative clauses and another for embedded nonfinites ('Equi-NP-deletion'), which is sensitive to the presence of an 'identical' noun-phrase in the context. This analysis misses the generalization that subjects can be absent only if the verb is nonfinite, as it is both in embedded nonfinite clauses and in imperative clauses. However, it has other problems too: the usual problems of identity (for example, in 'Nobody likes to lose', the subject of *to lose* mustn't be *nobody* in deep structure) and recoverability (in some cases there is no identical noun-phrase in the environment: cf. 'Selling drugs is illegal', 'It's fun to sing Christmas carols', 'Getting ourselves out of this mess is going to be difficult', 'It was very bad luck to lose her way like that', where the 'understood' subject of the embedded clauses is, respectively, *one, one, we* and *she*). Instead of introducing a subject and then deleting it, we can prevent the grammar from ever introducing it, by means of the function-assignment rules for SUBJECT. FU.1 defines the types of clause in which SUBJECT is present, either obligatorily or optionally; and FU.4 says that if SUBJECT is absent, then the nominal which would be SUBJECT, if this function were present, is also absent—we might say, it is 'suppressed' rather than deleted. This may seem a rather cavalier approach to rule-writing, but I see no reason a priori why a grammar shouldn't contain such a rule, and it surely corresponds exactly to the facts. Moreover, it is quite explicit and suitable for inclusion in a generative grammar.

The seventh type of deletion rule is the kind associated with conjunction—conjunction-reduction, gapping and right-node raising. There are numerous controversial issues connected with these rules, and all I can do is present the daughter-dependency equivalent of the transformational analysis which I advocate in Hudson (1976*b*). In this paper I argue for an analysis very similar in spirit to the one in Stockwell, Schachter and Partee (1973), in which the result of applying conjunction-reduction to a structure like fig. 18(*a*) is one like fig. 18(*b*).

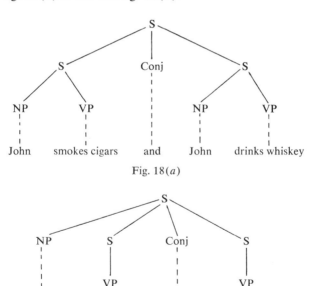

Fig. 18(*a*)

Fig. 18(*b*)

Now the easy way to handle constructions like these in daughter-dependency is by means of the kind of rules we used for raising: we show that *John* is a daughter not only of the top sentence but also of each of the lower ones. The only oddity about the rules we should need for this is that they would have to in some way apply 'across the board', but there is no problem in principle about this. The kind of structure we might generate, then, would be like fig. 19.

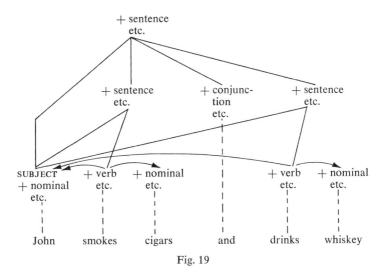

Fig. 19

There are many loose ends to be tied up here, such as the correct structure for coordinate structures, which here I have treated in terms of daughter-dependency throughout. However, it should be clear that it is quite possible that a viable daughter-dependency analysis could be worked out for conjunction-reduction—and that it wouldn't require deletion rules. Similarly I believe gapping can be handled without deletions, even in a transformational grammar (as I argue in the paper referred to). As for 'right-node raising', this raises so many problems for any theory that it is best left out of the picture at present. (For instance, it isn't restricted to coordinate structures: as witness 'Nobody likes, although most people agree to pay, the taxes that any modern state has to levy in order to support the services that its population have now come to expect'.)

Finally, there is relative-pronoun deletion, the rule which deletes a relative pronoun (presumably *that*) in nonsubject position inside the relative clause, giving '(the book) I bought', and so on. This may seem a trivial rule—and indeed, in a transformational grammar, it raises no matters of general importance at all. However, it is the hardest of all the deletions for a daughter-dependency grammar to handle, although I believe a satisfactory solution is possible. One possibility would be to treat it as we treated the subject: assume that the function of the deleted pronoun is TOPIC, and simply allow TOPIC not to occur in some clauses. Then it could be said that items which would be normally assigned to TOPIC are suppressed if there is no TOPIC. This approach encounters problems, however, in that there is no reason for the object of a sentence to be combined with TOPIC anyway, so if there's no TOPIC in a relative clause, the object will simply not move forward, and thereby avoid being suppressed. Moreover, the constraint on the suppression of TOPIC is odd: it may be suppressed only if it is *not* combined with SUBJECT, the one function that we have seen *does* allow suppression. Generally, the analysis would be unrevealing at best.

There is an alternative analysis, but it involves so many major questions that I can do little more here than outline it. It involves a completely new approach to relative clauses as a whole, with a new conception of the relation of the clause to its antecedent. Basically, we should allow *raising* out of relative clauses, and treat the use of relative pronouns as an alternative to this. Take the noun-phrase 'the man who I saw': this would have a fairly conventional analysis, with *who* as a daughter of the clause (introduced, incidentally, by daughter-dependency rule DD.7, and with the function RELATOR assigned to it by FU.11). If we now turn, however, to its 'reduced' equivalent, 'the man I saw', we should analyze this as having *the man* as a *daughter* of the relative clause, but also as its *sister*—just as for raised subjects and so on, as we saw in 3.8. According to this analysis, then, there would be no need to think of anything at all as being 'deleted', or even 'understood'—everything is as overt as in any raising construction. We now bring *that* into the analysis: if a nominal has been raised out of the relative clause, *that* may be added at the start of the nonraised part of the clause (just as in cases like 'What do you think *that* she does?'). But there's a difference according to whether the raised nominal is SUBJECT or not in the relative clause: if it is SUBJECT, *that* is obligatory; if not, it is optional.

This analysis has a lot of attractions, though it also has problems. To start with the latter, why is it that *that* is obligatory if the SUBJECT is raised, when this is precisely the condition under which it is *excluded* in the kind of raising resulting from wh-movement (cf. *'Who do you think that will come?')? Second, what are we to do with cases like 'nobody I know'—are we to say that the object of *know* is *nobody?* Given that this is a purely syntactic analysis, this may be possible, but one anticipates more problems from this source.

Turning now to the advantages of the proposed analysis of relative clauses, we find it has several. First, this analysis makes it natural that neither 'zero' (i.e. raising without *that*) nor *that* can occur after a preposition (*'the chair on that/∅ he was sitting'): the prepositional phrase can't be raised into the position of the antecedent, since this is reserved for noun-phrases, so raising isn't possible, and consequently *that* isn't possible either. Second, and similarly, the restriction on relative clauses in appositive positions becomes natural, if we think in terms of the raising analysis: the relation of an appositive relative clause to its antecedent is, in some respect, unsuitable for the raising analysis (maybe the relation is too loose or indirect); therefore not only the 'zero' pronoun but also *that* are excluded from appositive clauses. Third, Perlmutter has shown (1971: 99; Berman 1974) for French that the words *qui* and *que,* as they are found in relative clauses, should be treated as complementizers rather than relative pronouns, so that relative clauses containing them in fact lack a subject or object; this analysis looks remarkably similar to the one I am suggesting for English *that,* except that Perlmutter doesn't suggest the raising part of the analysis. (Nor is it clear how he would deal with other 'relative pronouns' than *qui* and *que.*) Finally, it is easy to extend the raising analysis to cover 'pseudorelative clauses', such as 'What he bought (weighed five pounds)': here *what* seems to act as both relative pronoun and antecedent—like a compressed version of *that which.* Now if the antecedent itself may be both a sister and a daughter of the relative clauses in cases like 'the man I saw', we can give the same analysis to *what* in 'what he bought', with the reservation that it belongs to a class of nominals which can occur only in this position.

Schachter (1973) has suggested an apparently similar transformational analysis of relatives, in which the noun-phrase which ends up as the antecedent starts off in deep structure embedded in the relative clause, and the latter has *no* noun-phrase as sister in deep structure—all it has is an empty node, into which the relevant noun-phrase will later be moved, leaving a copy (a relative pronoun) in the relative clause. For all its similarities to the analysis I have proposed, there are two fundamental differences. First, in Schachter's analysis *all* relatives involve raising ('promotion', in his terms), whereas in mine only some do; because of this, Schachter has no way of using his raising analysis to explain the similarities between 'zero' pronouns and *that,* as mine does. Second, for Schachter all relative clauses have the same deep-structure antecedent, namely, an empty node, whereas in my analysis there is no need for empty nodes, since the antecedent is treated as both a sister and a daughter of the relative clause in the same structure. One consequence of Schachter's analysis is that 'the boy who kissed the girl' and 'the girl who the boy kissed' will have the same deep structure—a consequence which many transformational linguists would, I think, find unacceptable.

The point of this discussion of relatives has been to introduce a possible way of handling 'relative-pronoun deletion', by showing that it isn't a case of deletion at all. It illustrates a principle which will be very evident in the next chapter: that the development of a new theory may well involve the development of new analyses of the facts as well.

4   Auxiliary Verbs

In this chapter, we shall be looking at one particular area of English syntax to see how it can be handled in daughter-dependency terms, and what advantages there are in trying to use daughter-dependency grammar rather than transformational grammar in describing it. The area of syntax for this chapter is the one that centers around the auxiliary verbs and their relation to the main verb, but the analysis I shall offer in fact covers a much wider area than this, including adjectival predicates and several types of 'catenative' verb (that is, verbs that take a nonfinite construction as complement but that are not auxiliary verbs by the usual criteria, such as *seem, think, try* and *persuade*). I shall assume that the term 'auxiliary' covers the following words (when used as auxiliaries in the usual sense of the term):

> (*a*)   aspectual auxiliaries: *have, has, had, having; be, am/is, are, was, were, being, been; haven't, isn't,* etc.
> (*b*)   passive auxiliary: *be,* etc.
> (*c*)   dummy auxiliary: *do, does, don't, doesn't, did, didn't*
> (*d*)   modal auxiliaries: *can, could, may, might, shall, should, will, would, must, ought, used, need, dare, am, is, are, was, were; can't,* etc.

The criteria by which these words are grouped together in contrast with nonauxiliary verbs are well known (see for example, Palmer 1965: 20): they all invert with the subject in interrogative clauses, they all have a corresponding form with *-n't,* they all (when finite) take emphatic stress and they all occur in elliptical clauses such as tag questions.

4.1. The Chomsky Analysis

In *Syntactic Structures* (1957: 111), Chomsky proposed an analysis of auxiliary verbs in which all the auxiliary verbs in a sentence are brought together under a single node, labeled Aux. The rule for expanding this node was

Aux $\longrightarrow$ C (M) (have + *en*) (be + *ing*)

where C stands for 'concord' (= later 'T' for 'tense'), and M stands for 'modal'. With minor changes, this analysis dominated the transformational scene exclusively until 1969, when Ross published his objections (to which we shall refer extensively below), and still appears to be the one favored by many transformational linguists. It is the basis for the analysis given in Burt's (1971) introductory textbook, for instance, and since this more recent analysis is better than the original one in a few minor respects, I shall take it as representative of the Chomsky analysis. For a sentence such as 'John may have been swimming', the deep structure would be like fig. 20.

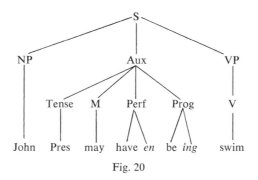

Fig. 20

This analysis has many shortcomings, and most of them have been pointed out by other linguists before me (Ross 1969*a*, Darden 1973, Huddleston 1974 and Borkin and Peterson 1972), so we can pass over it quite quickly. I shall just focus on three particular problems: the fact that auxiliary verbs are not in fact classified as verbs, the fact that all the auxiliary verbs are treated as making up a single constituent (Aux), and the fact that every sentence is considered to have a tense formative in its deep structure.

As Ross has pointed out (1969*a*), if you don't treat auxiliaries as verbs then you miss a number of generalizations which should apply to them as well as to main verbs. One generalization he mentions is that the rule of 'gapping' deletes material that must include 'the verb', where 'the verb' covers both main verbs and auxiliaries:

Harry invited Mary and Bill ~~invited~~ Susan.
Harry will sing and Bill ~~will~~ play the piano.

(In fact one can be more precise about the verb that must be deleted: it must be the *first* verb in its clause, regardless of whether this is a main verb or an auxiliary; Hudson 1976*b*.) Another generalization one could make is that *en* and *ing* are suffixes that are attached to verbs; but according to the Chomsky analysis, *be* isn't a verb, so we find ourselves in the odd situation of having a suffix which in some cases (e.g. . . . *have taken* . . .) is attached to verbs, and in other cases is attached to nonverbs (e.g. . . . *have been taken* . . .), but in *both* cases is introduced by the same rule. Moreover, the only way in which the 'affix-hopping' rule can be made to work is by having a general convention which will interpret M, *have* and *be* as verbs, along with main verbs—which amounts to an admission that the generalization about suffixes being attached to the next verb in the string just can't be made in terms of the Chomsky analysis, since this kind of convention clearly has no place in a transformational grammar. And finally, there are several rules for which one needs to be able to refer to 'the first verb' (or 'the finite verb', which in deep structure amounts to the same thing), but the only way in which one can do this (barring some kind of convention for adding 'verb' where necessary) is to form a disjunctive set containing M, *have, be* and Tense—but since it is exactly the *same* disjunctive set that is relevant for each rule (negative placement, subject-verb inversion and tag-formation), a generalization is clearly being missed.

Could this flaw in the Chomsky analysis be remedied by changing the phrase-structure rules so that they *do* classify the auxiliaries as verbs, without making any other serious change in the analysis? The answer is no, because the only way in which this could be done would be by having V dominating M, *perfect* and *progressive,* as in fig. 21.

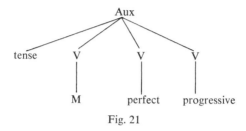

Fig. 21

(If V were dominated by M and so on, instead of dominating them, there would have to be a separate phrase-structure rule for each of these nodes, attaching just one node, V, under it, as well as the rule allowing V to be dominated by VP, and this would be entirely contrary to the spirit of phrase-structure rules, as I'm sure every transformational linguist would agree.) But if V separates M, *perfect* and *progressive* from Aux, there is no way in which the phrase-structure rule for Aux (or any other rule, for that matter) could get them in the right order (preventing, for example, a structure with M after *have* from being generated). This illustrates the very general weakness in transformational theory that it provides only one kind of rule (the phrase-structure rule) to show three different kinds of relation among constituents: classification (in this case, classifying elements as verbs or nonverbs), sequence and constituency. In other words, transformational grammar is based on the hypothesis that the classification of an element that is needed for stating its sequence relative to its sisters will always be the same as, or at least no less general than, the classification needed for any other purpose in the grammar. The question is whether this hypothesis is compatible with the facts about English auxiliaries; at least as far as Chomsky's analysis is concerned, there seems to be no way of reconciling the facts with the hypothesis.

The second problem with Chomsky's analysis is that it involves the constituent Aux, which brings together all the auxiliaries in a sentence. So far as I can see, there is no justification whatever for this constituent, and I know of no serious attempt to justify it. One assumes that the original reason for introducing Aux was that this was the best way available of showing that modals, *have* and *be* were auxiliaries, but it does not do this, of course—modals aren't shown to be auxiliaries by virtue of the Aux node dominating them any more than determiners are shown to be noun-phrases by having NP dominating them. If all the auxiliaries *do* form a constituent between them, then this is a very different type of constituent from noun-phrases, prepositional phrases and embedded clauses, the paradigm examples of constituents: the auxiliary constituent is interrupted much more freely by adverbials of various types (cf. 'John has, I think, been working too hard'), and auxiliaries can be deleted one at a time by conjunction reduction, whereas for all other constituents the rule is that they can be deleted only when they are daughters of the conjuncts in the particular coordinate structure concerned (Hudson 1976*b*).

> John has come home and ~~John has~~ been working for
>   two hours.
> *The boy came in and ~~the~~ girl went out.

Unlike the first flaw in Chomsky's analysis, this one can easily be remedied, simply by abandoning the constituent labeled Aux, and introducing all the auxiliaries directly as daughters of S. The deep structure for 'John must have been swimming' would then look like fig. 22.

The only disadvantage of this analysis, compared with the original Chomsky analysis, is that it doesn't give the impression that auxiliary verbs are being classified as auxiliaries; but as we have

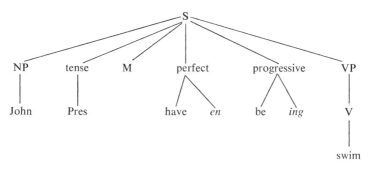

Fig. 22

just seen, this is only a false impression as far as the original analysis is concerned, so it is just as well to have an analysis which doesn't mislead.

The third fault with the Chomsky analysis (which it shares, incidentally, with the Ross analysis, as we shall see) is that it is based on a very suspicious morphological assumption: that every finite verb contains a tense suffix, even where this suffix is regularly unrealized in the phonology. We discussed this point in some detail in 2.4, but to recapitulate the argument, I said that even if there is justification for the segment labeled past, there is none for the one labeled present, except that postulating it makes the Chomsky analysis appear more convincing than it really is. One implication of analyzing, say, *look* as having no suffix at all in 'They look nice' would be that it would no longer be possible to group all finite verbs together, in contrast with infinitives and participles, by referring to the former as verbs bearing the tense suffix (and similarly for the distinction between 'tensed' and other clauses which looms so large in Chomsky's analyses, as in Chomsky 1973). Now that syntactic features are well established in transformational grammar, it is clearly much more attractive at first sight to reject the original Chomsky analysis in favor of one in which past-tense verbs have the feature [+ past], present-tense ones [– past], and both have the feature [+ finite], in contrast with the nonfinite forms. But this solution isn't in fact available in the transformational framework: the phrase-struc-

ture rules would have to introduce the feature [+ finite] separately from the verb node to which it has to be attached, since
the rule is that it's attached to whichever verb is the first in the
clause, whether this is an auxiliary or a main clause. Presumably
this would mean having a deep structure in which, say, [+ finite,
– past] is attached to something like an empty node to the left of
all the verb nodes, and a transformation for attaching these features to the first verb; but both the phrase-structure rule for introducing the features and the transformation for moving them
would have to be of a type otherwise unrecognized in transformational theory.

Before leaving the Chomsky analysis, I ought to mention a
variant of it which, according to Lightfoot (1974), has been
proposed by Emonds. In this analysis, Aux still exists, but it
dominates only T and (optionally) M; 'Perf' and 'Prog' would
be attached in deep structure to the verb-phrase, as in fig. 23.

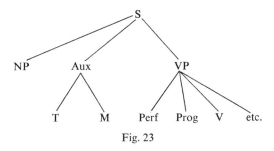

Fig. 23

If there is no modal, the first of Perf and Prog is raised transformationally into Aux. The main advantage of this analysis, of
course, is that 'Aux' now represents just the first auxiliary, rather
than all the auxiliaries as in the old analysis, so that rules like
subject-verb inversion can refer simply to 'Aux' instead of 'Tense
plus any of M, *have* or *be* that may be immediately after it'. Otherwise, however, it suffers from the same faults as the old analysis; in particular, it fails to treat auxiliaries as verbs, and it is
based on a doubtful morphological analysis of finite verbs.

4.2. The Ross Analysis

The revision that Ross suggested in 1969 was essentially that auxiliary verbs should be treated in deep structure as higher verbs —each one being the only verb in a sentence dominating an embedded sentence containing the next verb to the right. The main contribution of this analysis is to have treated auxiliaries as verbs without having recourse to general conventions for interpreting them as verbs for the sake of particular transformations. As an example of a structure based on Ross's analysis I quote the following from Darden (1973), rather than any of Ross's own few examples, since the latter raise irrelevant problems. Fig. 24 shows the deep structure for 'John has smoked pot'.

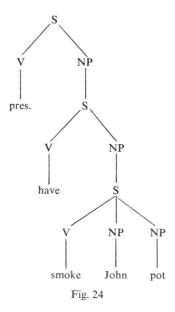

Fig. 24

This analysis has problems too, the main and most obvious one (though hitherto unnoticed, I believe) being that the label NP over the complement-sentence can't be justified. First, although auxiliaries can take *which* and *so* instead of a complement-clause, as Ross points out (cf. ' . . . , which he may'; ' . . . , and so may John'), the test of pseudocleft-sentences shows that the complement is not a NP:

    *What John may is be late.
    *What we have is gone to the pictures.
    *What they are is coming tomorrow.

Similarly, the complement can't be replaced by *it* (although it can be replaced by *that,* especially if the *that* is topicalized):

    . . . That he may.
    . . . *He may it.

And second, the verb-forms in the complement are all wrong for nominal sentences: if anything, they are the forms characteristic of *adjectival* clauses rather than of nominals. In particular, the passive participle is normal as the first verb in a reduced relative clause (cf. '[the man] chosen for the job') but never as the first verb in a nominal clause; and the *ing*-form participle never has progressive meaning except in reduced relative clauses and after *be* (and a few other verbs such as *keep*). In other words, if these complement-clauses are to be treated as NPs, the range of complementizers for clauses dominated by NP will have to be widened to include a range of others, particularly the -*en* suffix. (Notice that this problem can't be solved by having *to be* in the deep structure between the auxiliary and the next verb, so that the latter will depend on *be* rather than on the surface auxiliary, because it would then be virtually impossible to show which auxiliaries required which verb-forms, and in any case such deep structures would make no sense at all semantically.) Moreover, at least the passive participle and the progressive participle commute much more easily with adjectives than with NPs after *be:*

    He is working hard/busy.
    He is paid well/well paid.

(see Freidin 1975 for passive participles as adjectives). At the very least, it seems that there is doubt as to the status of at least some of the complement-clauses as NPs; but if they are not NPs, what can they be, in a transformational analysis such as Ross's? NP is after all what they *have* to be, since the deep structures would otherwise contain sentences containing a V but no NP at all.

Another problem with Ross's analysis is that it prevents us from stating the restrictions on the sequence in which auxiliaries can occur. It is true that structures like *'He is having finished' could probably be ruled out on semantic grounds (you can't have statives as the complement of the progressive *be*). But there is a genuine problem with the modal verbs, since there is nothing semantically wrong with, say, *'He has could/canned swim for a long time now', but modal verbs have to be prevented from following any other verb—except, in Ross's analysis, the 'tense' verb. However one tries to state this restriction there are problems. The most natural way is to say simply that modal verbs can't be nonfinite (i.e. they must be finite, either past or present); this automatically prevents modal verbs from being preceded by any other auxiliary, since a preceding auxiliary would require them to be nonfinite, but it would also explain why modal verbs can't occur in other nonfinite constructions, such as gerunds ('POSS-ING') and infinitives ('FOR-TO'):

*For students to can answer all questions is unusual.
*Musting go so soon is a nuisance.

But how could this restriction on the finiteness of modal verbs be stated in terms of the Ross analysis, given that every verb in deep structure, except for the very top one, is represented simply as a bare infinitive (i.e. as nonfinite)? Somehow the modal verbs would have to be prevented from being introduced under any V node except where the next V up the tree is the 'tense' V—a most unusual kind of restriction, to say the least. Moreover, this still wouldn't say anything about the other set of environments where modals are forbidden (in gerunds and infinitives), since these environments will presumably be created only later, by transformation, by which time it is too late to prevent modal verbs from being introduced; so a completely different restriction will have to be imposed on the relevant transformation (or, rather, transformations) whose effect will be exactly the same as that of the restriction on the deep-structure environments permitting modals: to prevent modals from being anything other than finite. Even if a solution could be found to the problem of restricting one verb in terms of the next verb up the tree, there would still be the equally serious problem of a major generalization being missed.

To be fair, there does seem to be one possible way out of this difficulty for advocates of the Ross analysis, although it would involve a small change in this analysis. If modal verbs were attached to the *same* node as the tense-features (or dominated by the same V node if tense were represented segmentally, as a morpheme), the distributional restrictions would be easy to state: each modal verb could be entered in the lexicon as obligatorily having the feature [+ finite] (or whatever the relevant feature was called), or as requiring tense as a sister. Moreover, the rules for creating gerunds and infinitives could be restricted so that they could delete the tense only if there were no modal verb attached to it, which would go some way toward explaining why modal verbs don't occur in these constructions. Whether the change involved in Ross's analysis would lead to other less acceptable complications I can't tell, but at least the problem of the finiteness of modal verbs would disappear, I believe.

A third problem with the Ross analysis is its dependence on a doubtful morphological analysis of present-tense verbs as containing a tense suffix. I discussed this problem in connection with the Chomsky analysis, so no more need be said about it here— except to point out that Ross's use of features on his V nodes, including features like [± past], isn't relevant, since the tense V is bound to remain as a separate segment right through to surface structure, given the operations that transformations are allowed to perform at present. The deep and surface structures for a sentence like 'Cows moo' will be something like fig. 25 (following Darden 1973 in not using features).

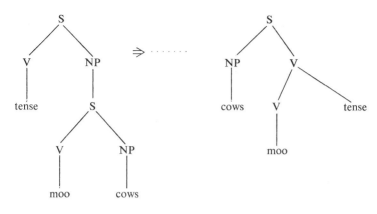

Fig. 25

The last problem with Ross's analysis to which I shall draw attention here also involves surface structure, and in particular the fate of the embedded S and the NP dominating it. In the structures just quoted, for 'Cows moo', I assumed that these two nodes would somehow have been pruned by the time surface structure had been reached—after all, by then both the nodes that were dominated in deep structure by the S would have been raised into the higher clause, so neither the S nor the NP over it would have anything to dominate. But what if something had been left over? There are two possible situations, one where just one element is left, and the other where more than one are left. The first situation arises, of course, wherever the embedded clause has just one NP or other node apart from the subject NP —as in 'Cows eat grass'. What should be the surface structure for a sentence like this? According to Darden's analysis, there would still be NP and S dominating the NP representing *grass,* but as he points out in a footnote, S-pruning should have taken place, so presumably the surface structure for 'Cows eat grass' would have no S over the NP for *grass*—but since there is no NP-pruning convention, there would still be a second NP over this NP, as in fig. 26.

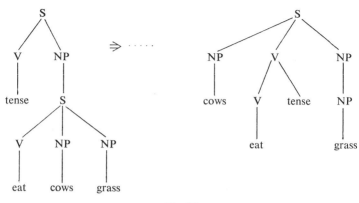

Fig. 26

It seems unlikely, to say the least, that this double NP analysis of *grass* could strike a naïve native speaker of English as intuitively satisfying—it is an artifact of the analysis, pure and simple. Now look at the surface structure for 'Cows eat grass well'. Here there would be *two* daughters for the embedded S after the subject and verb had been raised into the higher clause: *grass* and *well*. This being so, S-pruning doesn't take place, so the relevant deep and surface structures will be like fig. 27.

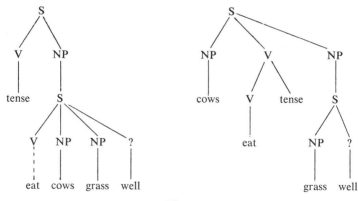

Fig. 27

We now have another major difference in the surface structures, involving this time the presence or absence of S; but all this reflects is the presence or absence of some element other than the direct object. A quick glance at the surface structures for 'Cows moo', 'Cows eat grass' and 'Cows eat grass well' shows how completely unrevealing the surface structures corresponding to Ross's proposed deep structures are.

We have described four shortcomings of Ross's analysis, of which three seem to be irremediable. We now turn to the daughter-dependency analysis of auxiliary verbs which, I believe, has all the virtues of both the transformational analyses, such as they are, and none of their vices. In a later section we shall broaden the scope of the discussion to show how the proposed analysis of auxiliaries fits into a more comprehensive grammar of English which allows for other types of verbs to be followed by nonfinite constructions.

4.3. The Daughter-dependency Analysis of Auxiliaries

Unlike Chomsky's analysis, we shall treat auxiliaries as a particular subclass of verb, but unlike Ross's analysis, we won't consider the verbs they 'take' to be in embedded complement-clauses. This means that for a sentence like 'John may have been swimming', the analysis identifies four verbs, the first three of which are auxiliaries and the last is not, and all four verbs will be sisters. Moreover, unlike both the transformational analyses, we shall show each verb except the first (*may*) to depend on the verb before it, not just for its form (*en*-form versus *ing*-form, and so on) but also for its very existence; in other words, there will be sister-addition rules which optionally add a further verb as sister to any auxiliary verb. The daughter-dependency structure for this sentence would look like fig. 28.

(For simplicity, I have omitted from this diagram the sister-dependency arrows leading to the subject, *John;* as a result of sister-dependency rule SD.1 and sequence rule S.9 this is a dependent sister of each of the four verbs, so there should be four separate arrows leading to it.) Unlike both the Chomsky and

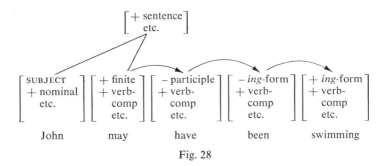

Fig. 28

the Ross analyses, this one treats auxiliaries as sisters of the main verb, whereas in Chomsky's analysis they are 'cousins' and in Ross's they are 'aunts'. In this respect my analysis is like that of Chapin (1973), though Chapin's reasons for preferring his analysis are different from the ones I shall offer.

I shall divide the discussion of this analysis into two parts, dealing with subcategorization and syntagmatic relations respectively. In the first part we shall have more points of comparison with Chomsky's analysis, since subcategorization was the weakness of that analysis, but in the second we shall focus on Ross's analysis, where most of the problems were syntagmatic.

First of all, then, there is the question of the classification of the auxiliaries, and in particular of how they are classified as verbs. The answer is simple: the class of verbs (+ verb) is divided into two unequal classes by the feature [± Aux], as in Ross's analysis. This is done by the classification rule for [+ verb], which simultaneously makes a number of other distinctions:

C.31 + verb: ± Aux

As for the feature [+ verb] itself, it is introduced by the classification rule for [+ predicate], which defines the class including both verbs and adjectives:

C.22 + predicate: ± verb

This means that any auxiliary is automatically covered by any rule which refers either to [+ verb] or to [+ predicate] (such as the rules that introduce non-initial verbs that we shall discuss below), as well as by rules that refer explicitly to [+ Aux] (such as the rules for inverting subjects and auxiliaries). Accordingly, Chomsky's problem of defining auxiliaries as verbs doesn't arise. However, the analysis also solves a number of other problems, including two problems involving the verb *have* which we didn't mention above. The first of these problems is that the auxiliary *have* can be used as an ordinary transitive verb, as in 'Have you a light?'. This is a problem for Chomsky, since he can treat *have* either as an auxiliary *or* as a transitive main verb, but not as both (in the analysis of a single sentence, that is); but for our analysis there is no problem, because the feature distinctions [± Aux] and [± transitive] are independent of one another, as can be seen from the classification rules for [+ verb] C.27 and C.31. The second problem is related to this: the transitive *have* may be used either as an auxiliary or as a nonauxiliary (I deliberately avoid using the term main verb in this context, for obvious reasons), since 'Do you have a light?' is also possible. For Chomsky, the two *have*s would be no more closely related than the two *can*s ('He can can anything with that canning machine'), but in mine they would differ in only one respect: one has [+ Aux], the other [– Aux].

On the matter of classification this analysis scores over Ross's analysis too, however, in that it solves the problem of the finiteness of modal verbs very simply, since modal verbs are prevented from ever being anything but finite by the organization of the classification rules: the feature [+ modal] depends on [+ finite] and [– perfect-comp], which characterizes modal verbs and the dummy *do:*

C.34 + finite, – perfect-comp: ± modal.

Not only does this rule prevent [+ modal] from ever combining with [– finite]; it also predicts (correctly) that *do* will always be finite.

Moreover, this analysis scores over *both* the others in that it doesn't depend on the assumption that present-tense verbs have a tense suffix: the distinction between past- and present-tense verbs is shown syntactically simply by the feature [± past] (C.36), and the question of how this feature distinction is realized morphologically is left open. The class of finite verbs is similarly defined by a feature [+ finite], whereas in Chomsky's analysis it is defined with reference to the morphemes past or present (subsumed under tense).

We now turn to the syntagmatic relations between auxiliaries and other verbs. One advantage of this analysis over Ross's is that it doesn't treat the 'complement' of an auxiliary verb as a noun-phrase—something which it manifestly isn't, as I showed above. Instead, the complement is simply a verb, as in the most traditional analyses. Another advantage is that the rule which introduces the complement can also specify the form of the verb required—for instance, there is a class of verbs with the feature [+ prog-comp], which include the auxiliary *be* (and also some nonauxiliaries, such as *keep,* as we shall see in 4.6), and which are subject to the sister-addition rule

SD.10 + progressive-comp⁻ → − passive

which says that such verbs take an *ing*-form verb as their complement (hence combinations like *be swimming, keep trying*). For Ross, there is one rule which introduces the second verb, and another which specifies its form; and, as we have seen, this second rule would be problematic in that the two verbs involved aren't clause-mates. In comparison with Chomsky's analysis, this aspect of the analysis counts as a point of superiority in that it allows a single rule to introduce both the *ing*-form after *be* and the one after verbs like *keep,* whereas in his analysis no such rule is possible, since, as we have seen, auxiliaries (*be*), and main verbs (*keep*) are completely unrelated categories.

On the matter of the relations between auxiliaries and their complements, the daughter-dependency analysis has three minor but interesting secondary advantages. First, it allows a very simple formulation of the 'doubl-*ing*' constraint (Ross 1972): no verb must be both [+ progressive-comp] and [+ ing-form] (a kind of feature-addition rule). This rules out all the cases where a progressive *ing*-form verb would follow (as a sister) another *ing*-form verb, as in *'Being working still at midnight is unusual for Bill' or *'Keeping hitting the wrong key is infuriating'. Unlike Ross's constraint, it has no difficulty in allowing cases like 'Avoiding hitting the wrong key is difficult', since in these cases the first *ing*-form verb is not [+ progressive-comp]; nor does it have any difficulty in ruling out cases where the progressive-taking verb has no complement (as a result, in transformational terms, of VP-deletion): in other words, 'John being surprised us all' can't be taken as the abbreviated form of *'John being working . . . ', although it can (I think) be taken as abbreviated form of, say, 'John being chosen surprised us all'.

The second incidental advantage of this analysis is that it makes it much easier to handle the kind of relations found in languages such as French and German, where different verbs take different auxiliaries in the perfect—for instance, in French *aller* 'go' takes *être* 'be' as its perfect auxiliary, whereas *marcher* 'walk' takes *avoir* 'have'. In this case the selection relation clearly goes in the opposite direction from the relation that determines the form of the second verb: from the second verb to the first. In Ross's analysis the second verb is in a lower clause than the first one (the perfect auxiliary), so at best a most unusual kind of rule would be needed to restrict the first (higher) verb to match the second—even if it were possible to overcome the problems raised by the fact that the perfect auxiliary in French can't be selected until after reflexivization has taken place (since all reflexive verbs take *être* as their perfect auxiliary). In the daughter-dependency analysis, on the other hand, the perfect auxiliary and the second verb are sisters, so there is nothing to prevent a sister-addition rule from adding appropriate features to the former (distinguishing *avoir* from *être*) according to the features of the latter.

Third, there are three combinations of an auxiliary plus a second verb in English which have idiomatic meanings and special syntactic restrictions: *have got* (meaning 'have'), *have been* (meaning 'have gone', as in 'I have been to Paris') and *be going to*. It seems necessary to analyze each of these combinations as an ordinary combination of an aspectual auxiliary plus participle

—for instance, it is just the first word that inverts in questions ('Have you got a minute to spare?'), and *be going to* is subject to the ordinary doubl-ing constraint which we discussed above (*'Being going to publish a book doesn't impress many people'). On the other hand, there are semantic and syntactic peculiarities of these combinations which must be included in the lexicon, one assumes—for instance, *have* must be finite in *have got* (*'He seems to have got wealthy parents'), and it is only in combination with *have* that *be* can mean 'go' (*'He was to London last week'). Although I don't know exactly how this kind of restriction should be shown in the lexicon, it seems self-evident that it's easier to show such restrictions if the verbs concerned are sisters than if they are in different clauses, as in Ross's analysis. Moreover, it seems that verbs can form such idiomatic groupings only if they are sisters; at least, there are no verb-verb idioms in English that I know of which wouldn't be treated, for other reasons, as sister-sister combinations in this analysis. In Ross's analysis, on the other hand, *no* verbs are sisters, so there would be no natural limit to postulate for idiomatic pairings of verbs.

A rather different type of advantage stems from the fact that later verbs are introduced by sister-addition rules, as dependent sisters of the preceding verb. This allows for a very simple treatment of so-called VP-deletion (as we saw in 3.9), generating sentences containing one or more auxiliary verb but no main verb or complements of the main verb ('He has', and so on): we simply make all the sister-addition rules in question optional. This means that once the first verb has been introduced (by a daughter-addition rule sensitive to the features of the clause, such as the rule that requires a finite verb in nonimperative main clauses, or an *ing*-form verb in gerunds), sister-addition rules can go on adding sister verbs to the right of it until either a verb is introduced that doesn't take sister verbs, or a voluntary stop is put to the chain. In other words, later verbs are never introduced, so they don't need to be deleted; moreover, the complements of the main verb won't be introduced unless there *is* a main verb, so they don't need to be deleted either. Thinking in terms of operations (rather than well-formedness conditions), we can see the derivation of a sentence like 'He must have been being given too much pocket money' as proceeding step by step:

He must.
He must have.
He must have been.
He must have been being.
He must have been being given too much pocket money.

At any step, the derivation can be halted, yielding a well-formed (elliptical) sentence.

In the following sections we shall look briefly at two particular auxiliary verbs—passive *be,* and 'dummy' *do*—to see how they are treated in this analysis, and then in the final section we shall see how the analysis spills over to cover various verbs other than auxiliary verbs.

4.4. Passives

Since one of the auxiliary verbs is involved in the passive construction, I ought to explain briefly how the other aspects of passives are handled in this grammar. In doing so I shall have a number of opportunities to point out further advantages of such a grammar over transformational grammars. Considering how large a place the passive transformation is given in most introductory textbooks on transformational grammar, it is surprising how unsuccessful transformational grammar has been in fact in formulating a satisfactory passive transformation and a satisfactory deep structure for passives. Indeed, the only transformational analysis of passives that I know of which comes near to being able to handle them satisfactorily is the one by Freidin (1975), which breaks away from the transformational tradition in having *no* passive transformation at all (see also, more recently, Langacker and Munro 1975). All the others that I know (Chomsky 1957, 1965; Hasegawa 1968; Burt 1971; R. Lakoff 1971) suffer from one or more of the faults in the following list:

(*a*) they require a transformation which will add an *extra* node for the passive auxiliary, such transformations

being problematic to say the least in transformational
theory (Bach 1974: 98);

(b) they require a similar transformation to add the *by* of
the passive, and to label *by* plus the NP moved over
from subject position as a prepositional phrase;

(c) they cannot prevent passive sentences from containing
verbs like *suit,* which take an 'object' NP but don't
passivize;

(d) they show no connection between *be* passives and *get*
passives;

(e) they involve deep structures in which two NPs (namely,
the subject of a higher sentence and the object of a
lower one) have to be the same—a restriction which
can't be imposed on context-free phrase-structure rules;

(f) they show no connection between the 'optionality' or
'deletability' of the agent prepositional phrase (*by* ...)
and that of virtually all other prepositional phrases
(but not noun-phrases) in the structure of the sentence;
nor do they show any connection between the fact that
the 'deep subject' changes into a prepositional phrase
and the fact that it has to leave the subject position and
move to the end of the VP, after all the other
noun-phrase complements.

Like Freidin's analysis, the daughter-dependency analysis that
follows suffers from none of these defects. On the other hand, to
the extent that Freidin's analysis is compatible with the rest of
transformational grammar, I can't claim that passive sentences
can't be handled in transformational grammar. What I *can* claim,
though, is that passives mustn't be used as evidence for the need
for transformations, as they have been in the past.

The relevant bits of the daughter-dependency grammar are
the following. First, *en*-form verbs are classified as either passive
[+ passive] or perfect [+ perfect] (see classification rules C.38
and 39). Although the verb-forms involved are the same in both
cases, the classes covered by [+ passive] and [+ perfect] are different: for instance, *suited* belongs to the one but not the other
(whence the impossibility of sentences like *'Her complexion
is suited by her new lipstick'). Next, there is the rule that intro-

duces [+ passive] verbs, as complements of [+ passive-comp] verbs (that is, of either the auxiliary *be* or a nonauxiliary like *get*):

SD.11 – progressive-comp$^\rightarrow$ + passive.

Since the complement-verb is more peripheral than the *be* or *get,* the order has to be *be/get* plus [+ passive]. The remaining sister-addition rules apply, adding any further complements that the second verb may need: one rule adds [+ nominal] for the feature [+ transitive]:

SD.2 + transitive$^\rightarrow$ + nominal

(not all passivizable verbs are [+ transitive], of course: for instance, *sit* and *sleep* can be passivized, as in 'This bed/chair has been slept/sat in'). And another rule adds the agent prepositional phrase:

SD.3 + passive$^\rightarrow$ + preposition (optional).

This rule needs a little explanation, so we shall digress briefly on the treatment of prepositional phrases in daughter-dependency grammar. This is something I've said little about so far in this book, because I'm not too sure how prepositional phrases should be handled, but as I have already suggested the best approach seems to be to treat prepositions and their objects as sisters, with the object depending on the preposition:

SD.17 + preposition$^\rightarrow$ + nominal

One advantage of this approach is that the preposition can be introduced directly by a sister- or daughter-addition rule, and this dependency can be shown easily in the lexical entries for the various prepositions. For instance, *by* can be shown as the only preposition with [+ preposition$^\leftarrow$ + passive] among its features. The main uncertainty as far as this analysis is concerned is whether the preposition and its complement noun-phrase should be treated as the only daughters of a larger unit, the prepositional phrase. If this does turn out to be necessary, there will be problems in generating the right structures with this kind of grammar.

Returning to the analysis of passives, let us see how the rules we have mentioned so far would generate a sentence like 'Frogs are eaten by Frenchmen'. For simplicity of presentation, we can pretend that the rules define operations, and take the operations one by one:

(*a*) Select features for the sentence node, and apply the daughter-dependency rule DD.1 and feature-addition rule FA.7 which between them give the sentence one compulsory daughter, a finite verb.

(*b*) Select features for this verb, including (obligatorily) [+ predicate] and (by free selection) [– progressive-comp].

(*c*) Apply sister-dependency rules to these features: SD.1 requires [+ nominal] as a sister for [+ predicate], and SD.11 requires [+ passive] as a sister for [– progressive-comp]; add the necessary sisters.

(*d*) Select features for the verb which has the feature [+ passive] which has just been introduced; again these will have to include [+ predicate], and may include [+ transitive].

(*e*) Apply the relevant sister-dependency rules again; this time, rule SD.1 does *not* require [+ nominal], because of the presence of [+ passive] (this is mentioned in a contextual condition on the rule), but SD.2 does require [+ nominal], as a sister for [+ transitive], and SD.3 requires [+ preposition] as a sister for [+ passive].

(*f*) Apply the sister-dependency rule for [+ preposition], SD.17, to add [+ nominal] as a sister to the preposition just added.

(*g*) Apply the peripherality-assignment rules to the complements of the verbs, taking each verb in turn; the finite verb has two, a nominal and a passive verb, but there's no peripherality ranking for these; the passive verb has three: a nominal, a verb and a preposition—again, no ranking.

(*h*) Apply the function-assignment rule for SUBJECT (we shall disregard the other functions), assigning SUBJECT to the least peripheral nominal complement of the least peripheral verb —which means the only nominal complement of the finite verb (the passive verb is more peripheral, being a complement of the finite verb).

(*i*) Apply the sequence rules as appropriate: S.7 puts SUBJECT first, S.8 puts the finite verb before the passive one, S.9 combines the (only) nominal complement of the passive verb with the (only) one of the finite verb (i.e. it says they both have the same subject), and S.11 puts all the dependent sisters after the elements on which they depend, except where the previous rules have specified a different order. The structure at this point (i.e. before we embark on generating structures for the nominals) is like fig. 29.

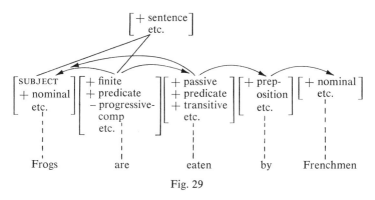

Fig. 29

The last point we need to discuss about this analysis is the absence of the [+ nominal] which normally depends on the feature [+ predicate]—in other words, the absence of anything corresponding to the 'underlying subject NP' of nearly all transformational analyses. In transformational analyses other than Freidin's it is assumed that the eventual subject of the active and the agent NP of the passive should be identified syntactically in deep structure—in other words, that they are the same syntactically. The difficulty is that the agent NP shows similarities not only to the active subject but also to other adverbial prepositional phrases: like the latter, it is optional, and follows NP complements. But if you show its similarities in deep structure to the active subject, you can't show its similarities, which are also relevant at deep structure, to other prepositional phrases, such as manner adverbials. Fortunately, it is easy to show its similarities to the active subject in the *semantic* representation, where both can be mapped onto whatever semantic elements (like 'actor') are relevant. Since it would be much harder to show similarities between the agent *by*-phrase and other prepositional phrases outside the level of syntax, I have opted for the alternative of showing the agent as a prepositional phrase in the syntax, and leaving the semantics to show its similarities to the active subject.

We have already seen how the *by* agent is introduced—by a sister-dependency rule for [+ passive]. All we need to do now is to prevent another nominal from being introduced as subject of passive verbs, and to do this we put a condition on the rule that introduces subjects, to prevent it from applying to passive verbs:

SD.1 + predicate→ + nominal/if not [+ passive]

(Notice that the condition has to be formulated like this, since the feature [– passive] refers to just the class of *ing*-form verbs.) A possible attraction of this analysis is that there are languages where no agent can be expressed in a passive clause (Beja, for instance), so for these languages a rule like this one would simply prevent the 'deep subject' from being introduced at all, rather than having it introduced and then obligatorily deleting it in all cases. Another attraction, of course, is that pragmatically one of the main uses of the passive is to avoid having to specify who the actor was, or even whether it was human or not (e.g. 'Our best sheets were ruined at the laundry'), as Sampson points out (1972).

4.5. 'Dummy' Auxiliaries: Do and Shall

In this section I shall discuss the phenomena covered in transformational grammars by the transformation called '*do*-support' or '*do*-insertion', plus a few others which involve *shall* rather than *do*. Even this transformation, which seems to be widely accepted among transformational grammarians, raises problems, such as the question of how *do* should be shown to be a verb (with, incidentally, exactly the same irregular morphology as the nonauxiliary *do*). However, there are no doubt ways of improving the rule within the transformational framework, such as the three ways suggested in 'Where the rules fail' (Borkin and Peterson 1972: 14), so I shall simply show how the phenomena concerned can be handled in my own grammar.

Broadly speaking, *do* is treated in this grammar in the same way as other auxiliaries: it is classified as an auxiliary with the feature [– modal], which means that like modal auxiliaries it must be finite; and it has the feature [+ verb-comp], which means that it is allowed to take another verb as complement. Like other auxiliaries, it can be placed before the subject (in questions, and after a preposed negative phrase such as *not only* and *at no time*); like other auxiliaries it can be negative, containing *-n't,* or can allow an 'external' negative *not* after it; and like other auxiliaries it can be used 'emphatically', to focus attention on the polarity (positive/negative) of the sentence. Consequently, the grammar will allow *do* to appear in just the same range of environments as modal verbs, and will do so by means of the same apparatus. However, there are three differences between *do* and other auxiliaries, including the modals, which the grammar has to reflect, by, among other things, restricting the environments in which *do* can occur, compared with other auxiliaries.

The first difference has nothing to do with syntax, and need not be reflected in the syntax in any way: *do* has no meaning. (This being so, it is rather surprising that the authors of 'Where the rules fail' are so happy to consider representing *do* in their semantic structure, alias deep structure.) To take account of this, all we need is a lexical entry for *do* which has nothing about meaning in it.

The second difference is that if *do* occurs directly before another verb (that is, not separated from the other verb by the subject or by *not*), and if *do* itself is positive (i.e. if it contains no *-n't*), then *do must* be emphatic—whereas all other auxiliaries may or may not be emphatic under these circumstances. This restriction can be handled fairly easily by imposing a special restriction on whatever rule introduces emphatic intonation, making it obligatory in the case of the features [– modal] (the feature that distinguishes *do* from all other auxiliaries) and [– negative]. If it is possible to relate this restriction to the fact that *do* has no meaning in itself (and therefore would add nothing to the communicative value of the sentence unless it was the bearer of some variable like emphasis or negation), so much the better.

The third difference is rather more complicated, since it involves the distinction between imperative and nonimperative sentences: in nonimperative sentences, *do* never occurs before another auxiliary. This restriction is easy to state, if we leave imperatives aside for the moment: whereas other [+ verb-comp] verbs determine the form of the next verb, *do* determines as well that its complement verb shall be a nonauxiliary. For this we need a sister-dependency rule for [– modal] (the feature which defines *do*):

SD.16   – modal$\rightarrow$ – Aux.

This prevents *do* from occurring before other auxiliaries by simply ensuring that the next verb won't be an auxiliary.

The complication lies in the fact that this restriction is relaxed for imperatives, as witness examples like 'Don't be silly!' and 'Don't be misled'. It would probably not be too difficult to reformulate the rule above to restrict it to nonimperative environments, but it would be preferable to try to find some reason *why* this odd restriction holds. The explanation seems to be that imperative sentences must contain an infinitive, by virtue of a feature-addition rule for [+ optative] (the feature which, in this grammar, defines imperative sentences):

FA.6   [item$_\leftarrow$ + sentence, + optative]: – participle.

But (I assume) the rule that introduces negative or emphatic verbs requires them to be finite auxiliary verbs, so if an imperative is negative or emphatic it will have to contain a finite auxiliary *as well* as the infinitive that it has to contain qua imperative. This is true even if the infinitive is itself an auxiliary, as in the examples just quoted, so we should expect a finite auxiliary to occur with the infinitive. Unfortunately I can't yet answer two questions: how best to restrict the finite auxiliary that occurs in such imperatives to prevent it from being anything other than *do,* and how best to introduce it in the first place. There are a number of possible answers, but until we have a proper analysis of negation and emphasis, it's too early to opt for one answer in preference to any of the others.

We can press this analysis further, entering an intriguing area of syntax which seems so far virtually unexplored: the area of imperative interrogatives. In standard transformational accounts of imperatives, they are assumed never to be interrogative (IMP and Q being mutually exclusive), but it can be argued that the following examples should all be treated as interrogative imperatives:

Shall I open the window?
Why don't you be quiet?
(I don't know) whether to go.

First, there is the behavior of *do* (or *don't*): in the second example, this occurs with the auxiliary *be,* as if the sentence were imperative. Second, there is the meaning of all three sentences, which in all cases defines some event which may or may not be desirable, much as in ordinary imperatives; and as far as the two main clauses above are concerned, they have, or at least can have, meanings very different from the 'ordinary' interpretation of the sentences as questions of fact—for instance, the 'Why don't you . . . ' construction refers to a single event in the future, rather than a habitual 'present' event. Assuming, then, that imperative interrogatives need to be allowed for, my grammar allows [+ optative] to combine with [+ interrogative].

This classification of the sentences above leads to two questions about their internal structures: why do the first two contain a finite auxiliary, and what determines whether this should be *do* or *shall?* The first question we can answer quite easily by referring to the daughter-addition rule which introduces a finite auxiliary if the clause is a non-embedded interrogative (with the feature [– nominal] to show that it's non-embedded):

DD.2 + interrogative, – nominal$_\rightarrow$, + finite, + Aux

One advantage of this rule is that it allows us to refer just to this auxiliary in the rule of subject-verb inversion, so that this rule need not refer to the features of the mother:

S.1 [+ finite, + Aux$_\leftarrow$ + interrogative, – nominal] $\rightarrow$ SUBJECT.

In other words, it is only the finite auxiliary introduced by the new rule that is put before the subject—and not the one which is present in all [– optative] clauses, whether embedded or not (hence the lack of inversion in embedded clauses). Furthermore, we now have an explanation for the fact that there is a finite auxiliary in both our non-embedded interrogative imperatives ('Shall I open the window?' and 'Why don't you be quiet?'): being non-embedded interrogatives they have to have a finite auxiliary, in spite of the fact that they are [+ optative]. This is the answer to the first question.

The second question is about the choice between *do* and *shall*. *Shall* can't occur in place of *do* in the 'Why don't . . . ' construction, and it looks as though *do* can't replace the *shall* in the other construction, though the data are less clear here (is 'Do I do it like this?' imperative?). Extending the range of examples shows that the only environment in which *do* but not *shall* occurs is after *why:*

Why/*when/*where/*what don't you eat?
*Why/when/where/what/$\emptyset$ shall we eat?

Of course there are other differences which are associated with the choice between *do* and *shall,* notably in the person of the subject. It may seem odd that *why* should be so different from other question-words, but it ties up with another odd fact about *why* noted by Quirk et al. (1972: 736): *why* is the only question-word that doesn't occur in embedded infinitive interrogatives:

I don't know *why/when/where/whether to eat.

This seems to confirm, in a rather unexpected way, that we should group together the *shall* constructions and the infinitive constructions, as [+ interrogative, + optative]; and since the former are in complementary distribution with the *do* construction, that should come in too. Be that as it may, the answer to the second question seems to be that *do* is used in interrogative imperatives only if they begin with *why* and are non-embedded; all other interrogative imperatives contain either *shall,* if they are non-embedded, or just the infinitival *to* if they are. How this set of constraints should be reflected, in detail, I don't yet know, but it is clear that the lexicon will have to allow *shall* as well as *do* to be the finite auxiliary required in interrogative imperatives.

To summarize this section, I have shown that there are two separate sources for the auxiliary *do:* on the one hand, it can be introduced under the same circumstances as any other finite verb, though it will have to be given emphatic intonation if it's positive and directly before the next verb; and on the other hand, it is the only finite auxiliary other than *shall* which occurs in imperative clauses, including interrogative imperatives of the kind just discussed. I don't feel that this analysis will have demonstrated any particular superiority of daughter-dependency grammar over transformational grammar, but neither do I feel that it has shown up any weaknesses of principle in daughter-dependency theory, since our grammar can handle at least the range of phenomena that '*do*-support' covers, and can do so in an insightful way with the possibility of extending the analysis to cover a whole new range of phenomena too.

4.6. Extending the Analysis

So far we have shown only how combinations of auxiliary plus verb are generated, but the grammar in Appendix 1 also covers several other constructions, involving nonauxiliary verbs such as *keep, get, grow, think, seem, know, say, make* and *sound.* Like auxiliary verbs, these can be followed by other verbs which depend on them, either directly or indirectly, but not all of them are like auxiliaries in allowing verbs as such as complements: some take adjectives or prepositional phrases (e.g. 'He kept happy/in a good mood'), and others take whole clauses, which may be introduced by *that* (e.g. 'I think that he's honest'), or

contain an infinitive (e.g. 'I believe him to be honest') or contain
no verb at all, but just an adjective, prepositional phrase or indefinite noun-phrase ('I believe him honest/in good form/an
honest man'). There are three directions, then, in which the
analysis can be extended: to cover nonauxiliaries that take verbs
as complements; to cover nonauxiliaries that take adjectives or
prepositional phrases as complements; and to cover nonauxiliaries that take clauses, of various types, as complements. The
aim of this section is relatively modest: just to suggest how the
analysis might be extended into these areas, and to show the kinds
of insight into the workings of the grammar that might be expected from the analysis. The area of grammar involving verb-
complementation is far too big and complicated for anyone to
be confident about being able to bring it all into his analysis, but
the small area that I shall discuss seems to present no great problems for daughter-dependency grammar. I shall not try to compare this analysis with the current transformational ones, since
this would require a whole book in itself—partly because there
are so many competing transformational analyses, and partly
because several of the differences between this analysis and transformational ones are descriptive rather than theoretical, and
would need more detailed discussion than could be justified in a
book on theory.

First, then, how can we bring in the nonauxiliaries which take
the same kind of verb-complements as auxiliaries? This is easy:
we simply add the verbs concerned to the lexicon, classifying
them with reference to the features already allowed by the classification rules in the grammar. Let us take just two verbs: *keep*
and *get*. Both verbs can take a progressive verb as complement,
so both must be allowed to have the feature [+ progressive-
comp], which is the one responsible for progressive verbs as
dependent sisters. Moreover, both verbs allow an object noun-
phrase before the progressive verb:

He kept/got moving.
He kept/got the wheel moving.

To allow for these two possibilities we allow both verbs to have either [+ transitive] or [− transitive] (whereas all the auxiliaries were [− transitive], at least when they had verb-complements). Finally, *get,* but not *keep,* can take a passive verb as complement, again with or without an intervening noun-phrase:

He got/*kept awarded a medal.
He got/*kept his friend awarded a medal.

The lexical entries for *get* and *keep* are very simple, and in neither case do they involve a disjunction of features:

get: − Aux, + passive-comp.
keep: − Aux, + progressive-comp.

(It can be seen from the classification rules (C.29, 30) that [+ passive-comp] subsumes [+ progressive-comp], rather than being incompatible with it as the names of the features might seem to suggest.)

One problem which these verbs may appear to raise is that of showing the relation between the object nominal and the verb-complement in sentences like 'He kept the wheel moving': somehow the grammar has to show that *the wheel* is subject of *moving* as well as being object of *kept.* In fact, however, this problem is solved by the sequence rule which we have already referred to (S.9), which says that the least peripheral complement of a dependent verb must combine with the most peripheral complement of the verb on which it depends. Any verb has at least one nominal complement (unless it is passive), by rule SD.1, so *moving* has one; and this is combined by the sequence rule just described with the most peripheral complement (i.e. the object) of *kept.* Accordingly, *the wheel* functions both as object of *kept* and as subject of *moving.* The structure will be like fig. 30.

It will be recalled from 3.7 that this sequence rule is also responsible for the relations between nominals and verbs like *try* and *persuade,* which are respectively [− transitive] and [+ transitive] according to this analysis. The structure for 'He persuaded the man to move' would be just the same as that for 'He kept the wheel moving', except that the features of *persuade* would be such as to require an infinitive as verb-complement rather than a

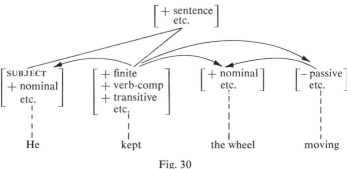

Fig. 30

participle (see the lexicon in section D of Appendix 1, and SD.14 and 18). As for verbs like *try*, they have only one nominal complement, their subject, so this is also their most peripheral complement and will be merged with the subject of the dependent verb by the same sequence rule. It can be seen how this rule allows daughter-dependency grammar to avoid the problems which transformational grammar faces in relating the subjects of *try* and its complement verb, as I pointed out in chapter 3.

This completes our discussion of the first way in which the analysis can be extended: it can be extended to allow various types of nonauxiliary verb to take verb-complements, just like the auxiliary verbs themselves. The first type is represented by *keep* and *get*—verbs which can take progressive and/or passive verbs as complement; and the second type is represented by *try* and *persuade*, which allow only infinitival complements, like modal auxiliaries. We have also seen that verbs which allow verb-complements add complements of their own to the stock of nominals in the sentence, and that one of these complement nominals has to be merged, or identified, with one of the nominal complements of the dependent verb.

The second direction for extending the analysis is toward sentences in which the complement is not a verb but an adjective or a prepositional phrase, like 'He kept quiet', 'He grew angry'. (I deliberately exclude indefinite noun-phrases from the list of possible predicates for reasons that will become clear shortly.) It is noticeable that participles and adjectives are very often inter-changeable:

> He kept them working/happy.
> He got talking/angry with a man he met.
> He had them finished/ready in an hour.

To show this distributional similarity, we can treat the verbs that allow such nonverbal predicates as a subclass of those that allow progressive predicates; so in the case of *keep, get* and *have,* there need be no explicit reference at all in the lexicon to the fact that they allow nonverbal predicates, since they all allow [+ progres-sive-comp], and this feature allows the features that lead to the presence of an adjective or a prepositional phrase (by SD.10a and 10b):

> C.30a + prog-comp, − Aux: ± nonverb comp.
> C.30b + nonverb comp: ± adj-comp.

Let us consider the verbs *keep, get, grow* and *be,* to see how they fit into this analysis. First of all, notice that of these verbs only *be* allows an indefinite noun-phrase as its complement:

> John was/*kept/*got/*grew a good linguist.

At first sight this restriction seems extremely odd, since on the one hand there is no semantic motivation for it (that I can see, at any rate), and on the other hand the syntactic relation be-tween the verb and the predicate looks the same in all cases. However, our analysis at least gives a *syntactic* motivation for the difference between *be* and the other verbs: *be* is the only aux-iliary in the group, and therefore it can't have the feature [+ non-verb comp] (according to rule C.30a). Therefore the predicates found with *be* can't be related to it in the same way as those found with the other verbs—and, as we shall see below, they are in fact part of an embedded clause, like the complements of verbs like *seem,* which do allow noun-phrases as well as adjectives and prepositional phrases. Our original list of four verbs (*keep, get, grow* and *be*) therefore contains only three genuine examples of verbs that take nonverbal predicates.

Of these three verbs, *grow* is different from the others in that the only complement it allows is an adjective—it doesn't allow a prepositional phrase or either kind of participle:

He grew angry/*in a temper/*shouting loudly/*put in a bad mood.

Consequently, we can identify it in the lexicon as obligatorily [+ adj-comp] (like *turn, wax, run* and so on). The other two verbs both allow either a prepositional phrase or an adjective, and both allow a progressive participle, as we have seen already, but *keep* doesn't allow a passive participle, whereas *get* does. To show these facts, all we need is the lexical entries that we gave above for *keep* and *get,* with *keep* as [+ progressive-comp], and *get* as [+ passive-comp]. Being able to show distributional facts as complicated as these without any disjunctions in the lexicon is very satisfying, and seems to vindicate the suggested analysis of sentences with adjectives and prepositional phrases as complements. (Another incidental source of support comes from the fact that verbs like *grow, turn, wax* and *run* seem to be linked collocationally to a limited range of adjectives each: one grows old, but one doesn't turn old, and so on. However this kind of restriction is to be stated, it will presumably be easier to state if it involves sisters than if the verb and adjective are as indirectly related as they are with verbs like *be* and *seem,* none of which shows this kind of collocational patterning.)

The third way to extend the analysis is to bring in constructions involving *sentences* as complements. The reason why we need to extend the analysis in this particular direction is that there are sentences which look as though they ought to be covered by the analysis we have already outlined, since they contain a verb with either an infinitive or a nonverbal predicate in its complement, but which nevertheless have nothing to do with the kind of sentence we have been discussing so far, since the complement of the verb is in fact a sentence rather than a verb, adjective or prepositional phrase. At this point we enter the field of sentential complementation, which is a vast area of grammar, so I shall just try to sketch in the bits of the grammar that cover the sentences that look most like the sentences we have been examining so far. To simplify the discussion I shall concentrate on verbs like *seem, sound, think, know, say, be* and *make,* and say nothing about volitional verbs like *want* or perception verbs like *see,* or any of the other types of verb which are discussed in detail in Hudson (1971).

The starting point for generating these constructions is the feature [± sentence-comp], introduced by the classification rule (C.21) for [+ predicate] (which covers adjectives as well as verbs, of course). All the verbs in the list above have the feature [+ sentence-comp], so all we have to do is first to classify the various types of sentence they take as complement, then classify the verbs themselves according to the types of sentence they allow and finally fit the two classifications together by means of dependency rules. (One problem we have already discussed is that the subjects of the embedded clauses are raised to act as subject of the main clause, unless the embedded clause is a full clause introduced by *that;* see 3.8.)

Let us look first at the classification of the complement-sentences. There are three types to distinguish: *that*-clauses (we shall ignore reported interrogatives, for simplicity), infinitives (with or without *to*) and verbless clauses, with an indefinite noun-phrase, an adjective or a prepositional phrase as predicate. Verbs like *think* and *consider* allow all three types:

I think that he's suitable.
I think him to be a suitable candidate.
I think him a suitable candidate/suitable/out-of-date.

Similarly, *seem* allows all three, though there is subject-raising (with discontinuity) with infinitives and verbless clauses, and extraposition with *that*-clauses:

It seems that he's suitable.
He seems to be suitable.
He seems a suitable candidate/suitable/out-of-date.

If all the verbs were like this, there would be no need to subclassify them beyond the feature [+ sentence-comp], but in fact many verbs don't allow all three types of complement. For instance, *know* is like *think* in taking *that*-clauses and infinitives, but doesn't allow verbless clauses:

I know that he's suitable/him to be suitable/*him suitable.

And *sound* is like *seem* in allowing verbless complements, but it doesn't allow *that*-clauses or (for me) infinitives:

*It sounds that he's suitable.
*He sounds to be suitable.
He sounds suitable/a suitable candidate/out-of-date.

Moreover, there are verbs that allow *that*-clauses but not infinitives or verbless clauses—for instance, *say* in the active:

They say that he's suitable/*him to be suitable/*him suitable.

Consequently we need to distinguish three verb-features, one for each of these complement types. We start by defining this general class of verbs as 'epistemic', because all but *be* and *make* are semantically epistemic, and then subdivide it:

C.23 + sentence-comp: ± epistemic
C.24 + epistemic, + verb: ± verbless-comp
C.25 − verbless-comp: ± *that*-comp.

Think and *seem* will be listed as simply [+ epistemic], since they allow the full range of complements; *know* will be listed as [− verbless-comp]; *sound* as [+ verbless-comp]; and *say* as [+ *that*-comp, *not* + passive] or [− verbless-comp, + passive].

The classes of complement-clause are also defined by features, of course, and the features concerned are those introduced in section B of Appendix 1. Rather than trying to justify this particular classification of clauses (which is only marginally relevant to the present chapter), I simply list below the features which identify the classes with which we are concerned:

that-clauses [+ nominal, − optative, − interrogative]
infinitives with *to* [+ nominal, − optative, − object-raising]
infinitives without *to* [+ bare]
verbless clauses [+ verbless, − relative]

I should point out that it would be very easy to extend the analysis to cover embedded interrogatives and 'subjunctives', found with verbs like *inquire* and *recommend* respectively, by using the features [+ interrogative] and [+ optative] respectively.

We can now give the sister-addition rules that relate the clause-classes that we have just distinguished to the verb-classes that we distinguished, namely, [+ verbless-comp], [+ *that*-comp] and [– *that*-comp]. (We didn't discuss there the possibility of some verbs taking bare infinitives, so we shall assume here that there are no such verbs, but note that verbs of perception are possible candidates.) The rules are very simple:

SD.5 + verbless-comp⁻ᐅ + verbless, – relative
SD.6 + *that*-comp⁻ᐅ + nominal, – optative, – interrogative
SD.   – *that*-comp⁻ᐅ + nominal, – optative, – object-raising

There are a number of aspects of the constructions in which the verbs already discussed occur that we haven't yet dealt with properly, such as the rules for extraposing *that*-clauses (see SD.16), but they would all take us far too deeply into the general question of how to treat sentential complements. Instead of extending the analysis even further in this direction, I should like to conclude this section, and the chapter, by looking again at the verb *be* (and a few related verbs).

When we discussed auxiliary verbs, in 4.3, *be* was one of the main verbs we dealt with, and I tried to show there that it was best to analyze progressive and passive complements of *be* as sister verbs, so that a sentence like 'John was being watched' would come out as a simple sentence. I then argued, in the second part of this section, that when verbs like *keep* take adjectives or prepositional phrases as complements, these too should be analyzed as direct sisters of the verb, so that 'He kept quiet' would be a simple sentence too. I pointed out, however, that this analysis would be wrong for other apparently similar verbs, such as *seem* and *be*, since these verbs, unlike *keep* and so on, can take an indefinite noun-phrase as complement. For *seem* it is relatively easy to argue for an analysis in which there is an embedded sentence—after all, *seem* allows *that*-clauses and infinitives, so it would be simpler to treat these cases as complex sentences as well. It is less obvious that all sentences containing *be* and a nonverbal predicate are complex sentences, so I shall now try to show why this analysis seems the best one to me.

The main reason is simply that verbless clauses are needed in any case because of a number of other environments, and that in all these other environments the range of items that can occur as predicate in the verbless clause is exactly the same as the range that can occur with *be:* indefinite noun-phrases, adjectives and prepositional phrases. We have already seen how verbs like *seem* and *believe* allow verbless clauses as complements, but there are other environments where verbless clauses occur. For instance, they can be introduced by *with* (which must be analyzed as a conjunction rather than a preposition, incidentally):

> With her parents so old-fashioned/out-of-date/
> archconservatives (it's not surprising that she's rather
> unadventurous herself).

There are several other types of adverbial environments in which verbless clauses can occur, with or without an overt subject, such as with *although* ('although old-fashioned . . . '), so if we can bring all these clauses together, and identify them also with the complements of *be* (or *become* or *make*), so much the better— especially since the alternative, as we have seen, is to treat *be* like *keep* and so on, and then have to explain why *be* allows noun-phrases and *keep* doesn't.

In connection with this point it is worth raising the question of whether a transformational analysis involving 'to-be deletion' might not be able to capture the same generalization, since one could postulate an underlying *be* or *to be* in all verbless clauses, and then just state the restriction on indefinite noun-phrases as a restriction on the application of 'to be deletion'. For instance, verbless clauses with *seem* and *believe* would be derived from underlying infinitives by this analysis. There are in fact a number of problems with such an analysis, apart from the general theoretical problem that deletions don't generally seem to be necessary, so deleting *be* would need that much stronger justification as a theoretical oddity. For one thing, not all *be*s can be deleted

—for instance, progressive and passive *be* can't be deleted after *seem,* as witness Chomsky's example of an ungrammatical sentence (1957: 75): **'The child seems sleeping'; and for another, there are a very heterogeneous range of environments in which to-be deletion would apply, as a glance at the examples discussed above will show, and it seems highly unlikely that it would in fact be possible to formulate a single transformation to cover them all.

In contrast with the above use of *be,* the existential and locative uses presumably don't involve embedded clauses, since they have to be alligned with verbs like *exist.* Instead, *be* will in these cases allow as complements first a nominal depending on the feature [+ predicate], and second the expletive *there,* depending on the feature common to all verbs that allow it—call it [+ existential]. Thus in a sentence like 'There was a lot of noise', *was* would in effect be treated just like an intransitive verb like *exist* or *arise,* except that [+ existential] would be obligatory for *be* but optional for the other verbs.

This brings the score of different uses of *be* to five: three uses with verbs as sisters (progressive, passive and modal), one use with a verbless clause as complement, and one use with just a nominal as complement. Each of these uses requires a different combination of features, the effect being that there is no way of referring to the verb (*be*) which occurs in them all by means of syntactic features—all they have in common is their morphology and, except perhaps for the existential and locative use, their lack of any meaning. *If* it turned out to be necessary to generalize syntactically about all the uses of *be,* as is often done in transformational grammar, this fact would of course count heavily against this analysis, and indeed against daughter-dependency grammar as a theory. However, I believe there isn't in fact any reason for generalizing across the uses, so the objection shouldn't arise. To justify this claim would take us further into the grammar—we should have to show, for instance, that wherever *be* has the expletive *there* as subject it is existential, in spite of apparent counter-examples like 'There were three men standing by the door' (where it looks as though *were* is progressive, with *standing* as a sister verb, as in 'Three men were standing by the door'). The claim can be justified, but once again we have to call a halt, otherwise we should be justifying a complete grammar for English (which, needless to say, I haven't yet got).

I think the most general point that will have emerged from this chapter (and the last sections of chapter 3) is that developments in linguistic theory must go hand in hand with developments in the descriptive analysis of languages. I make no apology for the fact that the daughter-dependency grammar for English that I have dipped into in this chapter can't be matched point by point against any existing transformational grammar, but makes completely different claims about syntagmatic and paradigmatic relations in sentence structure, as well as different claims about how the relevant structures should be generated. In a sense, the point of the chapter has been to show that there are areas of English syntax which need analyses which in principle can't be given within the transformational framework. I leave it to the reader to judge whether I have had any success.

5   Conclusions and Implications

I hope to have shown that daughter-dependency theory is at least a viable alternative to transformational grammar as a model for the syntactic part of language structure. In the course of the four chapters we considered a wide range of structures in English and I argued that for each of them daughter-dependency grammar is at least as good as transformational grammar and in many cases that it is much better. What this means, as far as syntactic theory is concerned, is that an adequate model of syntax does *not* need to include transformations, as has so often been claimed, and consequently that it doesn't need to generate more than one syntactic structure per sentence. To summarize the argument: it is possible to do without transformations provided one also does without phrase-structure rules; and instead of these two types of rule daughter-dependency theory allows for three main types of rule—for classifying, introducing and ordering elements respectively.

I have restricted the discussion so far more or less exclusively to syntactic structure, but it is possible to draw conclusions, however tentative, about other matters from these syntactic arguments, as the reader will no doubt have done already. The following are some of the implications that seem to me to follow from what we have said, but I offer them as speculations rather than as arguments.

First, as far as other levels of language are concerned, there are implications for both semantics and phonology. Assuming that the linguistic structure (the one generated by a generative grammar) ought to include some kind of semantic representation, it is clear that this must be different from the syntactic representation, since the latter is too concrete to show all the semantic facts that need to be shown. Moreover, if there are no transformations in syntax, the main argument for generative semantics collapses, since it can't be argued that the kinds of structure needed for semantics can be generated by using the transformations that are needed anyway for purely syntactic reasons (plus a handful of others). On the other hand, I think it is still an open question whether the 'separateness' of semantics and syntax lies in their needing separate structures, or whether they could perhaps be considered to be different aspects of the same structure, each giving a different range of information about the sentence, in terms of a different vocabulary of features.

For phonology, our conclusions about syntax raise the question of whether phonological rules such as are used in generative phonology have any more justification than their counterpart in syntax, transformation rules. I have to admit that the arguments for phonological rules for 'converting' a relatively abstract underlying form step by step into a relatively concrete one seem very strong, and it may well be that this is in fact the right way to do things in phonology. If this did turn out to be the case, it would be extremely interesting, of course, but the case for phonological mutation rules (Lamb 1964) at least needs reviewing in the light of the above criticisms of transformation rules.

Another consequence of abandoning transformations and the deep/surface distinction in syntax is that syntax looks much easier for the child to learn: apart from the obvious problems of segmentation and identification of items, the child's main task in processing adult language is to classify the items he hears, and identify the dependencies among them. Having done this, he shouldn't find it too hard to work out any changes that may be needed in his provisional grammar to take account of new types of sentences that he encounters. In particular, there is no question of reconstructing an abstract deep structure on the basis of a concrete surface structure, as in transformational grammar, where the child has to be able to both work out what the more abstract structures should be and identify the relations between the different structures at the same time. On the other hand, to say that the child would have an easier task in working out a daughter-dependency grammar for his language is in no way to deny the possibility, or indeed the probability, of his having linguistic universals of various kinds programmed into him from birth. I for one should be both surprised and disappointed if daughter-dependency grammar were a worse framework for the search for universals than transformational grammar has been.

Finally, one might draw similar conclusions about the mechanics of language processing—speaking and hearing. The lack of a distinction between deep structure and surface structure in syntax must inevitably make it easier for speakers and hearers to use daughter-dependency grammars than transformational grammars, since all they have to do is to construct a single syntactic structure, rather than a whole series of them. Accordingly, we might be more optimistic about finding psychological evidence for the reality of the structures we generate than one could reasonably be in transformational grammar.

To conclude, however, I should like to stress that I have been arguing throughout this book as a generative linguist, in trying to show that daughter-dependency theory offers a better basis for generative grammar than transformational grammar does. I have tried to play the same game as most transformational-generative linguists play, with the same criteria of success or failure, so it should be easy for other generative linguists to decide to what extent I have succeeded. Moreover, no doubt there are many faults in the version of daughter-dependency theory I have presented here; but it should be easy for other linguists who are already playing the generative game to improve on my performance.

Appendix One   A Partial Grammar for English

The following grammar includes all the rules that are referred to in the text, and some others that are needed to make these rules fit together; but there are large areas of English syntax which it covers either barely or not at all (notably, the noun-phrase, adverbial phrases and clauses, factive constructions and a number of construction-types which involve nonfinite verbs). The aim is to help the reader to get an overall view of the workings of a daughter-dependency grammar and to test the claim made in this book that such a grammar can generate a wide range of complex constructions which have hitherto been thought to need a grammar containing transformations to generate them.

I have tried to make the grammar as self-explanatory as possible, by annotating it in various ways. To explain the classification rules I have given either informal 'traditional' names, or specific examples, to show the classes defined by the various combinations of features generated by the rules; except in section D, which is a sample lexicon, the feature-combinations shown exhaust all the possibilities allowed by the grammar. The remaining types of rules are explained simply by giving a prose gloss on them, or by actually formulating them in ordinary prose where there is no formalism available. I must emphasize that the explanatory material is *not* part of the grammar, in order to prevent readers from forming a false impression of the length of the kinds of grammar written in terms of this model. Moreover, if any reader would like to compare the length of this grammar with that of some comparable transformational grammar, he ought to remember that the individual rules in this grammar are much simpler than those found in transformational grammars, so that a simple count of the number of rules won't give a fair comparison.

A. Classification Rules: Primary Classification

C.1–3   'item': ± sentence, ± phrase, ± nominal
as a network:

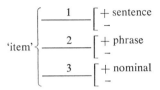

as a paradigm of features, with explanatory glosses:

+ sentence, + phrase, + nominal	gerund-clause (POSS ING)
– nominal	?
– phrase, + nominal	noun clauses other than gerunds (FOR TO, THAT, WHETHER, etc.)
– nominal	main clauses, relative clauses, participial clauses, infinitival clauses used as relatives
– sentence, + phrase, + nominal	noun-phrases
– nominal	adverbial phrases, prepositional phrases (?)
– phrase, + nominal	expletive *it, there*
– nominal	other words.

C.4–16   B. Classification Rules: Clauses

C.4,5   + sentence, – phrase: ± optative, ± moody
C.6   + moody: ± interrogative
C.7   + nominal, – moody: ± raising
C.8   + raising: ± object-raising
C.9   + nominal, – optative, + moody: ± mobile
C.10   – nominal, – moody: ± relative
C.11   – nominal, – moody, – optative: ± neutral
C.12   + neutral: ± verbless
C.13   + verbless: ± nom-pred
C.14   – nom-pred: ± adv-pred
C.15   + relative, – verbless: ± reduced
C.16   – relative, – verbless: ± bare

as a network:

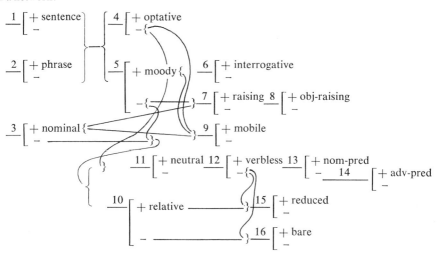

as a paradigm: (*a*) embedded noun-clauses (+ sentence, + nominal)

+ phrase	gerund-clauses
– phrase, + optative, + moody, + interrog.	*whether/how to do it*
– interrog.	*that he do it*
– moody, + raising,	
+ obj-raising	*it . . . (for him) to do*
– obj-raising	*he . . . to do it*
– raising	*(for him) to do it*
– optative, + moody, + interrog.,	*whether/how he*
+ mobile	*does it*
– mobile	*if he does it*
– interrog.,	
+ mobile	*that he does it*
– mobile	*he does it*
– moody, + raising,	
+ obj-raising	*it . . . (for him) to do*
– obj-raising	*he . . . to do it*
– raising	*(for him) to do it*

(*b*) main clauses (+ sentence, – phrase, – nominal, + moody)

+ optative, + interrog.	*(How) shall we do it?*
	Why don't you do it?
– interrog.	*Do it!*
– optative, + interrog.	*(How) does he do it?*
– interrog.	*He does it*

(*c*) 'adjectival' clauses (+ sentence, – phrase, – nominal, – moody)

+ optative, + relative	*(for him) to do*
	to do it
– relative	*to do (it)*
– optative, + relative, + neutral, + verbless, + nom-pred	*a fool*
– nom-pred, + adv-pred	*in a hurry*
– adv-pred	*silly*
+ neutral, – verbless, + reduced	*doing it* (not progressive)
– reduced	*who does it*
– neutral	*doing it* (progressive)
	done it (perfect)
	done (by him) (passive)
– relative, + neutral, + verbless, etc.	as above
– verbless, + bare	*do it*
– bare	*to do it*
– neutral	*doing it,* etc., as above

C.17–19   C. Classification Rules: Phrases

C.17   – sentence, + phrase: ± wh-phrase
C.18   – sentence, + phrase, + nominal: ± def-NP
C.19   – sentence, – nominal: ± conjunction

as a network:

as a paradigm (shared feature: [– sentence]):

+ phrase, + nominal, + wh-phrase, + def-NP	relatives (e.g. *who, that*)
– def-NP	interrogatives (*who, what*)
– wh-phrase, + def-NP	definite NPs (*the boy, he*)
– def-NP	indefinite NPs (*some boy, someone*)
– nominal, + wh-phrase, + conjunction	*whether* (?)
– conjunction	*how*
– wh-phrase, + conjunction	*that*
– conjunction	?
– phrase, + nominal	expletive *it, there*
– nominal, + conjunction	*if*
– conjunction	other words

C.20–34   D. Classification Rules: 'Predicates' (Verbs and Adjectives)

C.20	– phrase, – conjunction: ± predicate
C.21,22	+ predicate: ± sentence-complement, ± verb
C.23	+ sentence-comp: ± epistemic
C.24	+ verb, + epistemic: ± verbless-comp
C.25	– verbless-comp: ± *that*-comp
C.26	– verb, – epistemic: ± obj-raising comp
C.27,31,32	+ verb: ± transitive, ± auxiliary, ± finite
C.28	+ verb, – sentence-comp: ± verb-comp
C.29	+ verb-comp: ± passive-comp
C.30	+ passive-comp: ± progressive-comp
C.30a	+ progressive-comp, – Aux: ± nonverb comp
C.30b	+ nonverb comp: ± adj-comp
C.31,32	(see C.27 above)
C.33	+ Aux, – passive-comp: ± perfect-comp
C.34	– perfect-comp, + finite: ± modal

as a network:

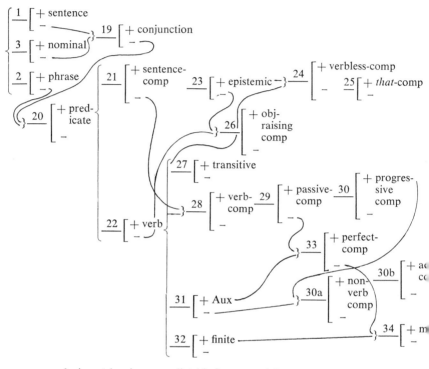

as a lexicon (showing unpredictable features only):

likely	– verb, + epistemic
probable	– infin-comp
normal	– obj-raising comp
easy	– epistemic, – verb
pretty	– S-comp
believe	– Aux, + transitive
know	– verbless-comp, – Aux, + transitive
want	– epistemic, – Aux, + transitive
hit	– sentence-comp, – Aux, + transitive
break	– sentence-comp, – Aux
seem	+ epistemic, – Aux, – transitive
sound	+ verbless-comp, – Aux, – transitive
happen	– epistemic, – Aux, – transitive
fall	– verb-comp, – Aux, – transitive
be (copula)	+ verbless-comp, + Aux, – verb-comp, – transitive

be (passive/	
progressive)	+ passive-comp, + Aux, – transitive
be (modal)	+ modal, – transitive
do (aux)	– modal, – transitive
keep	+ progressive-comp, – Aux
get	+ passive-comp, – Aux
grow	+ adj-comp, – Aux
have (perfect)	+ perfect-comp, – transitive
have (possess)	– sentence-comp, + transitive
have	
(experience)	– sentence-comp, – Aux, + transitive
may	+ modal, – transitive
try	– passive-comp, – Aux, – transitive
persuade	– passive-comp, – Aux, + transitive

C.35–39   E. Classification Rules: Verb-forms

C.35   + Aux, + finite: ± neg-Aux
C.36   + finite: ± past
C.37   – finite: ± participle
C.38   + participle: ± perfect
C.39   – perfect: ± passive

as a network:

as a paradigm (shared features: [– sentence, – phrase, – nominal, – conjunction, + predicate, + verb]):

+ Aux, + finite, + neg-Aux, + past	*wasn't*
– past	*isn't*
– neg-Aux, + past	*was*
– past	*is*
– finite, + participle, + perfect	*been*
– perfect, + passive	——
– passive	*being*
– participle	*be*
– Aux, + finite, + past	*took, suited*
– past	*takes, suits*

– finite, + participle, + perfect	*taken, suited*
– perfect, + passive	*taken*
– passive	*taking, suiting*
– participle	*take, suit*

C.40–45   F. Classification Rules: Words Other Than Predicates

C.40,41   – predicate: ± article, ± noun
C.42,43   + article: ± definite, ± wh
C.44   + noun: ± plural
C.45   – article, – noun: ± preposition

as a network:

as a paradigm (shared features: [– sentence, – phrase, – nominal, – conjunction, – predicate]):

+ article, + noun, + definite, + wh, + plural	*who, that*
– plural	*who, that*
– wh, + plural	*they*
– plural	*he*
– definite, + wh, + plural	*who* (?)
– plural	*who, what*
– wh, + plural	*some*
– plural	*some, somebody*
– noun, + definite, + wh	*whose*
– wh	*the*
– definite, + wh	*what*
– wh	*some*
– article, + noun, + plural	*boys*
– plural	*boy*
– noun, + preposition	*by, to*
– preposition	*to* (with infin.)

DD.1–11   **G. Daughter-dependency Rules**

Rules for clauses:

DD.1   + sentence→ item

> Every clause contains one item whose features reflect the features of the clause (see feature-addition rules FA.1–7).

DD.2   +interrogative, – nominal→ + finite, + Aux

> Non-embedded interrogatives contain a finite verb.

DD.3   + sentence→ – nominal (optional)

> Any clause may contain any number of 'sentence' adverbials. (This rule is almost certainly wrong.)

DD.4   + interrogative, + nominal→ –sentence

> Any embedded interrogative is introduced by *whether, if* or an interrogative 'pronoun'.

DD.5   + moody, + optative, + nominal→ + phrase

> Any embedded 'imperative' is introduced by *that, whether* or an interrogative 'pronoun'.

DD.6   + mobile→ + phrase

> Any 'mobile' embedded clause is introduced by *that, whether* or an interrogative 'pronoun'.

DD.7   – reduced→ + wh-phrase

> Relative clauses are introduced by a relative 'pronoun'.

Rules for phrases:

DD.8   + phrase, – sentence, + nominal→ + noun

> Noun-phrases contain a noun or pronoun as head.

DD.9   + wh-phrase→ + wh

> Wh-phrases contain a wh-word.

DD.10   + def-NP→ + definite

> Definite NPs contain a definite article or a definite pronoun.

DD.11   – def-NP$_\rightarrow$ – definite

> Indefinite NPs contain an indefinite noun or pronoun.

SD.1–18   H. Sister-dependency Rules

Rules for general complements of predicates:

SD.1   + predicate$^\rightarrow$ + nominal/*not* + passive

> Every verb or adjective takes one nominal as complement, provided it isn't passive.

SD.2   + transitive$^\rightarrow$ + nominal

> Transitive verbs take another one.

SD.3   + passive$^\rightarrow$ + preposition (optional)

> Passive verbs optionally take *by* as complement (and *by* takes a nominal as its own complement—see SD.17 below).

Rules for sentential complements of predicates:

SD.4   + sentence-comp$^\rightarrow$ + sentence, – phrase

> Some verbs and adjectives take a sentence (other than a gerund) as complement.

SD.5   + verbless-comp$^\rightarrow$ + verbless, – relative

> This sentential complement may contain no verb,

SD.6   + that-comp$^\rightarrow$ + nominal, – optative, – interrogative

> Or it may be a clause introduced by *that* or nothing,

SD.7   – that-comp$^\rightarrow$ + nominal, – optative, – object-raising

> Or it may contain an infinitive with *to,* and a raised subject.

SD.8   + obj-raising comp$^\rightarrow$ + object-raising, + nominal, – optative

> Some adjectives take an infinitive with its object raised ('tough-movement');

SD.9   – obj-raising comp$^\rightarrow$ – raising, + nominal, – optative

> Others take an ordinary infinitive clause.

Rules for predicates as complements of predicates:

SD.10   – nonverb comp→ – passive

> Some verbs take an *ing*-form verb as complement,

SD.10a   + adj-comp→ – verb

> Others take an adjective,

SD.10b   – adj-comp→ + preposition

> Others take a prepositional phrase,

SD.11   – progressive-comp→ + passive

> Others take a passive (*en*-form) verb,

SD.12   + perfect-comp→ + perfect

> Others take a perfect (*en*-form) verb,

SD.13   – perfect-comp→ – participle

> Others take a bare infinitive verb

SD.14   – passive-comp, – Aux→ – preposition

> And others take *to* plus an infinitive.

SD.14a   – modal→ – Aux

> Auxiliary *do* doesn't take another auxiliary as complement.

Rules for raising, extraposition and prepositional complements:

SD.15   + raising→ + nominal

> Some clauses have their subjects or objects raised to act as their sisters (see function-assignment rules for SUBJECT and TOPIC, in section J below).

SD.16   + moody, + nominal→ + nominal, – phrase,
          – sentence/ if there's no other [+ nominal]
                    as verb-complement (optional)

> If an embedded *that*-clause or interrogative clause is the only nominal complement of the verb, it may have *it* as an extra sister (to act as subject); the clause is then extraposed by the peripherality and sequence rules.

SD.17 + preposition→ + nominal

Prepositions take nominals as complements.

SD.18 – preposition→ – participle

'Infinitival' *to* takes an infinitive as complement.

FA.1–11 I. Feature-addition Rules

Rules for relating the clause's predicate or predicative phrase to the clause's own features:

FA.1 [item← + sentence, + nom-pred]: – def-NP

Some clauses have an indefinite NP as (first) predicative element,

FA.2 [item← + sentence, + adv-pred]: + preposition

Others have a prepositional phrase,

FA.3 [item← + sentence, – adv-pred]: – verb

Others have an adjective,

FA.4 [item← + sentence, + phrase, + nominal]: – passive

Others have an *ing*-form verb (a gerund),

FA.5 [item← + sentence, + reduced]: – perfect

Others have an *ing*-form or *en*-form participle,

FA.6 [item← + sentence, + optative]: – participle

Others have a bare infinitive;

FA.7 [+ verb]: + finite

Otherwise verbs are finite (unless required to be nonfinite by sister-dependency rules SD.10–14).

Rules for selecting a 'complementizer'

FA.8 [+ phrase, – sentence← + interrogative, + nominal]: + wh-phrase

In an interrogative clause, the complementizer may be *whether* or an interrogative 'pronoun'.

FA.9 [– phrase, – sentence← + interrogative, + nominal]: + conjunction

Or it may be *if*,

FA.10   [+ phrase← . . . – interrogative]: – wh-phrase,
                                                                          – nominal

                              Or in a declarative clause it is *that*.

Rule for preferring main clauses to subordinate clauses:
FA.11   [item]: – nominal, + moody

                              Normally (i.e. unless there are struc-
                              tural pressures to the contrary) items
                              are 'main' clauses.

FU.1–9   J. Function-assignment Rules

Rules for SUBJECT:
FU.1   SUBJECT is *present* as daughter of [+ sentence] if

      (i)   another daughter is [+ finite]
                              I.e. a finite verb needs a subject.
   or (ii)   [+ sentence] is [+ optative, – interrogative,
                + nominal]
                              I.e. 'subjunctive' clauses (e.g. '(I rec-
                              ommend) that John be appointed')
                              need a subject.
   or (iii) [+ sentence] is [+ relative, – optative]
                              I.e. relative clauses, other than infini-
                              tives, need a subject.
   or (iv)   [+ sentence] is *not* [+ optative], with another
                daughter as TOPIC, *nor* [+ object-raising,
                + nominal, – optative]; if only condition (iv) is
                satisfied, SUBJECT is optional.
                              I.e. otherwise, subjects are optional,
                              except that they're excluded in em-
                              bedded or main imperative clauses
                              with a front-shifted object, and also
                              where the object is raised, by 'tough-
                              movement'.

FU.2   If it's present, SUBJECT is assigned to the least
   peripheral nominal complement of the least peripheral verb
   in [+ sentence].

FU.3   If [+ sentence] is [+ raising], the raised nominal
   (see SD.15) must be SUBJECT (within the [+ raising]
   clause), provided this clause is not [+ object-raising].

FU.4   If SUBJECT is *absent,* the nominal to which SUBJECT
   should be assigned is also absent from any structures in
   which it would otherwise be required.

Rules for TOPIC:
FU.5   TOPIC is *present* as daughter of [+ sentence] if

(i)   [+ sentence] is [+ moody]

I.e. clauses which show mood allow a complement to be front-shifted.

or (ii)   [+ sentence] is [+ object-raising]

I.e. if the object is raised, it must be counted as TOPIC.

FU.6   If TOPIC is present it is assigned optionally

(i)   to a [+ wh-phrase] daughter of [+ sentence] (whether or not it is a verb-complement), provided [+ sentence] is [+ interrogative];

or (ii)   to any complement of the predicate(s) in [+ sentence], except for those that are [+ wh-phrase];

or (iii)   to a *constituent* of a sentential complement of the predicate(s) in [+ sentence], subject to the above constraints on [+ wh-phrase]. (I.e. topics and interrogative pronouns may be 'raised' into the structure of some higher clause, not necessarily the next one 'up'.)

FU.7   If TOPIC is separate from SUBJECT, TOPIC must be more peripheral than any other complements in the same clause.

FU.8   If an item in an embedded clause has the function TOPIC with respect to a higher clause, according to (b.iii) above, it must also be TOPIC in its own (i.e. the embedded) clause.

FU.9   If [+ sentence] is [+ object-raising], the raised nominal (see SD.15) must be TOPIC within the embedded clause.

Rules for RELATOR:

FU.10   RELATOR is *present* as daughter of [+ sentence] if any of the items to which it can be assigned is present.

FU.11   RELATOR is assigned, obligatorily,

(i)   to any relative 'pronoun' [+ wh-phrase, + def-NP] inside [+ sentence], whether this is daughter of [+ sentence] or not (i.e. relative pronouns can be 'raised'),

or (ii)   to any conjunction [+ conjunction],

or (iii)   to the interrogative element (*how,* etc; *whether; if*) introducing an embedded interrogative clause [– sentence←, + interrogative, + nominal],

or (iv)   to the element (*that, whether, how,* etc.) introducing embedded 'imperative' clauses [+ phrase← + moody, + optative, + nominal],

or (v)   to the *that, whether* or *how,* etc. introducing 'mobile' embedded clauses [+ phrase← + mobile].

S.1–12   K. Sequence Rules

Rules referring to specific features:

S.1   [+ finite, + Aux← + interrogative, – nominal] ⪢
SUBJECT/if SUBJECT ≠ TOPIC

> I.e. the finite verb in a main inter-
> rogative clause precedes the subject,
> provided that this isn't also the topic
> (as in 'What happened?').

S.2   SUBJECT ⪢ [– Aux]

> I.e. if a verb precedes the subject, it
> must be an auxiliary verb.

S.3   [+ finite] = [+ finite]

> I.e. if a finite verb is required by more
> than one rule in the same clause, it
> must be the same verb in both cases
> —in other words, only one finite verb
> is allowed per clause.

S.4   [+ verb] ⪢ [– mobile]

> I.e. an 'immobile' clause (introduced
> by *if* or zero) must follow all verbs
> in the clause.

S.5   [+ article] ⪢ [– article]

> I.e. articles precede nouns.

*Rules referring to functions but not to
specific features:*

S.6   RELATOR ⪢ TOPIC ⪢ SUBJECT

> I.e. these three functions may co-
> occur on the same node, or occur on
> different nodes, in the sequence
> shown.

S.7   Items with functions precede items without functions.

Rules referring to peripherality (see also FU.2):

S.8   Less peripheral items precede more peripheral items
(subject to S.1–7).

S.9   The least peripheral complement of a dependent verb
should be combined (on the same node) with the most
peripheral complement of the verb on which it depends
(e.g. subject of *try* = subject of dependent verb; object of
persuade = subject of dependent verb).

S.10   The most peripheral nominal complement of the
'higher' verb should be combined with any raised subject or
object [+ nominal ← + raising] or with expletive *it*
[– sentence, – phrase, +nominal ← + moody, + nominal].

Rules referring to dependency:

S.11   If one item depends as a sister on another, the two
should be adjacent (subject to S.1–10), and the dependent
one should follow the other.

S.12   If feature A presupposes feature B (in the classification
rules), then any features depending as sisters on A should
be combined, where possible subject to other rules, with
features depending as sisters on B.

Appendix Two

Daughter-Dependency Grammar and Standard 'Dependency Theory'

1. Dependency Structure and Constituent Structure

Two views of syntactic structure have dominated the last three or four decades: the one which emphasizes part-whole relations, and the one which emphasizes dependency relations among the parts. The first is typically American, with Leonard Bloomfield as its father figure, and underlies all the main American schools of syntactic theory (so-called immediate constituent analysis, transformational grammar, stratificational grammar and tagmemics)—and also, incidentally, other versions of 'systemic' grammar. The second is typically European, and stems from the work of Tesnière; it thrives at present, especially in Germany, under the name of dependency theory (with 'valency theory' as a name for some of the most important parts of the general theory). For the sake of a name, we can refer to the first approach as the constituency approach and to the second as the dependency approach. A number of attempts have been made to incorporate parts of one theory into the other—for instance, Robinson (1970) Anderson (1971) and Heringer (1970) represent attempts at synthesizing a theory in which both types of structural relations are shown, though the attempts are very different from one another. Daughter-dependency theory, described in this book, is another attempt to bring the two approaches together, and this is the justification for the present appendix.

The main difference between the two is that the constituency approach recognizes syntactic units of various sizes, with larger ones consisting of one or more smaller ones, while in the dependency approach there is only one size of unit (which, for simplicity, we can call the word—leaving open the possibility of breaking words down into morphemes). To take a simple example, the sentence 'The dog barked' would be analyzed as containing the following syntactic units according to the constituency approach:

1. the dog barked
2. the dog
3. the
4. dog
5. barked

That is, there are five different units to be classified and five units to be related to one another. In the dependency approach, on the other hand, only the last three of these units would be treated in the grammar, so that in principle terms like 'sentence', 'clause' and 'phrase' will have no place in a dependency grammar. Each approach has developed a way of using treelike structures to reflect syntactic relations within sentences: phrase-markers for the constituency approach, and 'stemmas' (Tesnière 1959) for the dependency approach. Leaving the question of labels aside, diagrams for 'The dog barked' would be like fig. A.1.

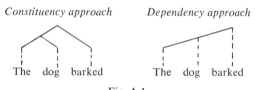

Constituency approach   *Dependency approach*

The   dog   barked   The   dog   barked

Fig. A.1

The use of tree-diagrams in both approaches can be misleading, since the vertical axis has very different meanings: in constituency diagrams, it shows size or, more accurately, the relation between a whole and its parts (the whole is higher than its parts), whereas in dependency diagrams it shows dependency, and *not* a part-whole relation, with heads being higher than the elements depending on them. For instance, in the constituency approach *dog* is shown as a part of the phrase *the dog,* and this is shown by the vertical line connecting the node representing *dog* to the node representing *the dog;* in contrast with this, the line going up from the node representing *dog* in the dependency diagram connects it to the node representing *barked,* and there is no sense in which *dog* is meant to be taken as part of *barked.* Using the usual terminology (developed in terms of the constituency approach), one approach shows relations (by means of connecting lines) between mothers and daughters, but not between sisters; while the other approach shows connections between sisters, but not between mothers and daughters (since, it claims, there *are* no mothers). In the following, I shall use the terms 'mother' and 'daughter' only for the part-whole relation, and shall use the term 'sister' even when one of the items concerned depends on the other. It leads to nothing but confusion to use the mother-daughter terminology to refer to the relations shown in a dependency diagram of the standard type shown above.

Robinson (1970) has shown that dependency structures and constituency structures are formally equivalent, in the sense that one can be converted in a mechanical way into the other, though she argues that dependency structures have certain advantages over constituency structures (in particular, they show directly which elements are heads and which are dependent on them). She recommends that a kind of dependency structure should be used, instead of the familiar phrase-markers, in the base of a transformational grammar; but the kind of structure she recommends is in effect a dependency structure which has been translated into a constituency structure, without however losing the information about the distinction between heads and modifiers. In other words, she shows how one can see dependency structures as constituency structures.

What I have argued for in this book is the converse of this approach: I have, in effect, argued for seeing constituency structures as dependency structures. The bulk of the argument is to be found in chapter 3 ('Structure-building Rules'). First I argued that some relations between daughters and their mothers could best be seen as dependency relations between individual features of some daughter and individual features of the mother: the former are allowed to be present only by virtue of the fact that the latter are present. Similarly, leaving aside the question of features on higher nodes, one can easily translate a phrase-structure rule such as

NP $\longrightarrow$ Det N

into dependency terms: Det and N, the daughters, are allowed to be present only when NP is also present (this is compatible with the definition of dependency in Hjelmslev 1961: 23, where

Hjelmslev explicitly allows for dependencies between parts and wholes). And second, I argued (or rather assumed) that some relations between sisters involve direct dependency of one on the other, notably in the case of verbs and their complements. Having made these two assumptions, one can take the argument a step further: not all daughters need to be related to their mother directly, but only those that are directly dependent on the mother; others can be shown as depending just on some other sister, and ultimately, more or less indirectly, on the mother. Moreover, some daughters can be shown as depending directly both on the mother and on some sister. The result is a kind of structure in which all dependency relations are shown directly, but in which constituency relations are shown only indirectly; in other words, not all of a mother's daughters will be connected to it by a single line, as they are in a constituency diagram.

The name of the theory, daughter-dependency grammar, is meant to reflect the properties of the structures which the grammars generate. The 'dependency' part is clear, given the above discussion; and the 'daughter' part is put in to distinguish this theory from standard dependency theory, in which all dependency relations are between sisters, rather than between a daughter and its mother. No name is ideal, and the snag with this one is that it depends for its significance on the distinction between mother-daughter relations and sister-sister relations made above, a distinction which I find others find less obvious than I do.

2. Attractions of the Dependency Approach

The dependency approach has stimulated some interesting developments in syntactic theory, notably (in my estimation) the work of Heringer (1970), Vater (1975) and Werner (1975), not to mention the large descriptive literature based on valency theory, applied mainly to German. What are its attractions? Here I can only draw attention to the features which appeal to me, and point out that the other advocates of dependency theory mentioned above (and in the previous section) have other reasons for favoring the dependency approach.

The most obvious attraction is that where one item depends on a sister, this dependency can be shown directly. This is particularly helpful in describing the relations between types of verb

and the complements they can take—the classification of the
verb determines the kinds of complement (noun-phrases, clauses,
adjectives and the like) that can occur with it, and only these are
introduced, by the relevant sister-dependency rules (or their
equivalent in dependency theory). In a constituency-based grammar, on the other hand, any relations there are between the verb
and its complements must be shown either via the classification
of the mother or via the lexical-insertion rules. The former approach is typical of other versions of systemic grammar, and a
glance at the complexities of my own earlier grammar (Hudson
1971, especially pp. 244–45) is enough to encourage one to look
for alternatives. The approach via lexical-insertion rules, and the
lexicon, is more typical of transformational grammars; here one
first generates some arbitrary structure containing some as yet
unspecified verb, and then selects from the lexicon a verb that
will fit the structure in question. The lexical-insertion rules have
to be able to inspect the contents of each lexical item, and check
it for compatibility with the complements—a role very similar to
that of our sister-dependency rules, the difference between the
two approaches being that in daughter-dependency grammar,
and dependency grammars in general, no other rules are needed
in the generation of verb-complement patterns, whereas in typical transformational grammars these patterns are generated directly by phrase-structure rules, and then again indirectly by the
lexical-insertion rules.

Apart from the increased simplicity of a dependency-based
grammar in the treatment of verb-complements, there are other
advantages. For instance, the category 'verb-complement' is self-
defining: a verb-complement is any item which depends on a
verb. In a transformational grammar, or any other type of constituency-based grammar, verb-complements aren't nearly as
easy to distinguish from other types of item—they may be defined
either as items dominated by VP (in grammars that contain VP
—unlike most grammars based on 'generative semantics') or as
items referred to in the strict subcategorization features of the
verb, which means that one has to consult the lexicon before
deciding whether or not some item is a complement. On the other
hand, it seems that it is useful to be able to refer to verb-complements, to the exclusion of other items; in the grammar in Appendix 1 there are several rules that do so, such as the rule for

assigning the function TOPIC (corresponding to the transformation of topicalization).

Another advantage of the dependency approach to complementation is that it greatly simplifies the lexicon, in the way pointed out in chapter 2, and generally simplifies the grammar as a whole. To take a simple example, there are a number of verbs in English—a very large number, in fact—that can occur either with an object or without one. Semantically, there are different relations between the sentences with and without the object, as can be seen from the following examples:

He was eating (something).
I know (something).
He was shaving (somebody).

(I do not mean to imply that *something* or *somebody* is 'understood' in all the objectless sentences, less still that it is in some sense present in their deep structures.) One approach, the transformational one, to such sentences is to assume that there is an underlying structure with an object present and that a transformation is responsible for the absence of the object in surface structure. This is the normal transformational analysis, and is associated with the use of 'rule-features', since some verbs allow the transformation to apply, and others (such as *say*) don't; so the derivation of the objectless sentences involves first generating a structure containing an object, then discovering a verb which can take an object, then deleting the object if the verb allows this deletion. Moreover, each of the three sentences above would have to have a different object in the underlying structure, since 'He was eating' means the same as 'He was eating something' but 'I know' doesn't mean 'I know something' but rather 'I know it (sc. what has just been mentioned)' and 'He was shaving' means 'He was shaving himself'; accordingly, either there will have to be three different transformations, each deleting a different item and sensitive to different rule-features on the verb, or there will have to be a very complicated transformation which deletes different items with different verbs. Clearly, there are problems with the transformational approach.

Using the dependency approach, at least if it is supplemented by classification rules to give a sophisticated classification of verbs, we find that a much simpler solution is possible: a contrast is made between [+ transitive] verbs, which cause a sister-dependency rule to introduce an object, and [– transitive] verbs, which don't; and verbs like *eat, know* and *shave* can be left unspecified as to the feature [± transitive] in the lexicon, so that they can easily occur either with or without an object. As for the semantic properties of the 'understood' object, if one is understood, this can be handled where it belongs, by the rules relating syntax to semantics. It then becomes clear why there are so many verbs like this in English: the more there are, the simpler the lexicon is, since fewer verbs need to be specified for [± transitive]. The 'derivation' of sentences like 'He was eating' is simpler than in the transformational analysis (as I have explained, in 1.2.2, the concept of 'derivation' makes sense only if rules are seen as operations rather than conditions on well-formedness): first you generate structures containing verbs with their syntactic features specified, but without any specific lexical item being selected as yet; then the sister-dependency rules apply, adding whatever complements are required by the features of the verb; and then (much later in the derivation, in fact) a particular lexical item can be chosen, to be compatible with the syntactic features specified.

Finally, the dependency approach has the advantage of being able to be extended to subsume the constituency approach, but not vice versa, since as I showed in the first section of this appendix the relations between mothers and daughters shown in a constituency-based analysis can be reinterpreted either as direct daughter-mother dependencies or as dependencies between sisters. This approach allows a clear distinction to be made between different kinds of dependency relations: for example, in a simple sentence with one verb the verb depends both for its presence and for some of its features (those that determine its form, as finite, an infinitive or a participle) on the features of the mother, whereas the complements other than subject have nothing to do with the features of the mother (unless the latter are used to reflect the 'transitivity' of the verb, as in other versions of systemic grammar), and everything to do with the features of the verb. As for the subject, it is related in both directions: for its presence, it is related to the features of the mother and also to those of the verb; and for certain of its features, it is related to the features of the verb. In contrast with both types of structure illustrated at the be-

ginning of this appendix, then, a daughter-dependency analysis
for 'The dog barked' would look like fig. A.2, again leaving the
labels off the tree.

Daughter-dependency structure

The   dog   barked

Fig. A.2

3. Disadvantages of Standard Dependency Grammar

It should be clear from the above that daughter-dependency
grammar isn't much closer to standard dependency theory than
it is to standard constituency theory, since it makes use of *both*
types of relation. I now have to explain why, given the attractions
of the dependency approach, I have rejected standard dependency theory.

The main reason is that in dependency theory proper there are
no 'higher' nodes, representing internally complex items (i.e.
mothers); and since there are no higher nodes, neither can there
be any features on higher nodes. In 2.3 I gave a number of arguments for attaching features to higher nodes, in order to be able
to cross-classify and subclassify clauses and phrases. If these
arguments are valid, then they prove that there must be higher
nodes, to represent the clauses and phrases that need cross-
classifying and subclassifying. It is true that dependency trees
can be interpreted in terms of phrases: 'A phrase consists of an
element plus all of its direct and indirect dependents' (Robinson
1970: 260). However, the only node to which the necessary features could be attached would be the one representing the head
of the phrase, and the whole point of our arguments in chapter 2
is that there is no element in a phrase or clause to which it would
be appropriate to add the necessary features. To take the relative-
clause example, there is no element within the surface structure
of all relative clauses that could be used in all cases as the bearer
of the feature [+ relative]: some relative clauses have a relative

pronoun, some don't; some have a participial verb, some don't; and in other respects they are just like other kinds of clause.

This decision not to allow nonterminal nodes leads to much the same consequences as the transformational decision not to allow discontinuities or features on higher nodes: the only way to cover all the syntactic information that needs to be given about a sentence's structure is to generate more than one structure for it, and relate them by transformation. In particular, it is necessary in any dependency grammar proper to postulate abstract underlying elements which have to be deleted before the surface structure is reached. To take a simple example, I know of two proposals for showing syntactic mood ('sentence type') in the dependency literature, and both of them involve abstract underlying elements. The original proposal was in Robinson (1970: 265), where an element T was proposed as the head of the sentence, with the verb (and subject) depending on it (see fig. A.3).

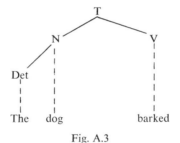

Fig. A.3

(Robinson's actual proposed structure differs from this in ways that aren't relevant to the present point.) The element T can then be used to bear features which show tense (hence the choice of name for the element) and mood (declarative versus interrogative). According to Vater (1975: 29), the element T should be reserved for tense, and mood should be shown instead by postulating an underlying performative verb, following the suggestions of Ross (1970). There are problems of a descriptive kind with either analysis: for instance, how do you justify the position of T in the underlying string, and how do you decide which of the many possible performative verbs has been deleted? But leaving these problems aside, we find that the only reason for having to postulate these underlying elements is that the initial assumptions about the nature of syntactic structure make them essential. As I have argued in the body of this book, changing these initial assumptions can make it unnecessary to postulate any kind of underlying structure, and therefore it may not after all be necessary to have transformations.

References

Anderson, J. M. 1971. *The Grammar of Case: Towards a localistic theory.* London: Cambridge Univ. Press.

Bach, E. 1974. *Syntactic Theory.* New York: Holt, Rinehart & Winston.

Baker, C. L., and M. K. Brame. 1972. Global rules: A rejoinder. *Language* 48: 51–76.

Berman, A. 1973. A constraint on tough-movement. *Chicago Linguistic Society* 9: 34–43.

Berman, A. 1974. On the VSO hypothesis. *Linguistic Inquiry* 5: 1–36.

Berry, M. 1975. *An Introduction to Systemic Linguistics 1: Structures and Systems.* London: Batsford.

Borkin, A. and D. Peterson. 1972. Where the rules fail: A student's guide. Distributed by Indiana University Linguistics Club.

Bresnan, J. W. 1970. On complementisers: Toward a syntactic theory of complement types. *Foundations of Language* 6: 297–321.

Bresnan, J. W. 1972. Theory of complementation in English syntax. MIT Ph.D. dissertation.

Burt, M. K. 1971. *From Deep to Surface Structure: An Introduction to Transformational Syntax.* New York: Harper & Row.

Chafe, W. 1970. *Meaning and the Structure of Language.* Chicago: University of Chicago Press.

Chapin, P. G. 1973. Quasi-modals. *Journal of Linguistics* 9: 1–10.

Chomsky, N. 1957. *Syntactic Structures.* The Hague: Mouton.

Chomsky, N. 1965. *Aspects of the Theory of Syntax.* Cambridge: MIT Press.

Chomsky, N. 1970. Remarks on nominalisation. *Readings in English Transformational Grammar,* ed. R. A. Jacobs and P.S. Rosenbaum. London: Ginn.

Chomsky, N. 1972. Some empirical issues in the theory of transformational grammar. In N. Chomsky, *Studies on Semantics in Generative Grammar.* The Hague: Mouton.

Chomsky, N. 1973. Conditions on transformations. *A Festschrift for Morris Halle,* ed. S. R. Anderson and P. Kiparsky. New York: Holt, Rinehart & Winston.

Chomsky, N. 1974. Questions of form and interpretation. *Montreal Working Papers in Linguistics* 6: 1–42.

Darden, B. J. 1973. On confirmative tag sentences in English. *Chicago Linguistic Society* 9: 104–13.

Davey, A. 1974. The formalisation of discourse productions. Edinburgh University Ph.D. dissertation.

Dougherty, R. C. 1970. A grammar of coordinate conjoined structures, I. *Language* 46: 850–98.

Downes, W. J. 1974. Systemic grammar and structural sentence relatedness. London School of Economics. Mimeo.

Emonds, J. 1972. A reformulation of certain syntactic transformations. *Goals of Linguistic Theory,* ed. S. Peters. Englewood Cliffs, N.J.: Prentice-Hall.

Fawcett, R. P. 1974. Systemic functional grammar in a cognitive model of language. West Midlands College of Education. Mimeo.

Fillmore, C. J. 1968. The case for case. *Universals in Linguistic Theory,* ed. E. Bach and R. Harms. New York: Holt, Rinehart & Winston.

Freidin, R. 1975. On the analysis of passives. *Language* 51: 384–405.

Haas, W. 1973. Review of J. Lyons, *Introduction to Theoretical Linguistics. Journal of Linguistics* 9: 71–114.

Halle, M. 1964. On the bases of phonology. *The Structure of Language,* ed. J. Fodor and J. Katz. Englewood Cliffs, N.J.: Prentice-Hall.

Halliday, M. A. K. 1961. Categories of the theory of grammar. *Word* 17: 241–92.

Halliday, M. A. K. 1967. Notes on transitivity and theme in English, part 2. *Journal of Linguistics* 3: 199–244.

Hankamer, J. 1973. Why there are two *thans* in English. *Chicago Linguistic Society* 9: 179–91.

Hasegawa, K. 1968. The passive construction in English. *Language* 44: 230–43.

Heringer, H. J. 1970. *Theorie der Deutschen Syntax.* Munich: Max Hüber.

Hjelmslev, L. 1961. *Prolegomena to a Theory of Language,* trans. F. J. Whitfield. Madison: University of Wisconsin Press.

Hochster, A. 1974. Verbal complements and lexical filtering. Distributed by Indiana University Linguistics Club.

Householder, F. W. 1971. *Linguistic Speculations.* London: Cambridge University Press.

Huddleston, R. D. 1974. Further remarks on the analysis of auxiliaries as main verbs. *Foundations of Language* 11: 215–29.

Huddleston, R. D., R. A. Hudson, O. E. Winter and A. Henrici. 1968. Sentence and clause in Scientific English. University College London. Mimeo.

Hudson, G. 1972. Is deep structure linear? *Explorations in Syntactic Theory,* ed. G. Bedell. *UCLA Papers in Syntax* 2.

Hudson, R. A. 1967. Constituency in a systemic description of the English clause. *Lingua* 18: 225–50.

Hudson, R. A. 1970. On clauses containing conjoined and plural phrases in English. *Lingua* 26: 205–253.

Hudson, R. A. 1971. *English Complex Sentences: An Introduction tc temic Grammar*. Amsterdam: North Holland.

Hudson, R. A. 1972. Why it is that that that that follows the subje impossible. *Linguistic Inquiry* 3: 116–19.

Hudson, R. A. 1973. Tense and time reference in reduced relative clau *Linguistic Inquiry* 4: 251–56.

Hudson, R. A. 1974. Systemic generative grammar. *Linguistics* 139: 5–

Hudson, R. A. 1975. The meaning of questions. *Language* 51: 1–31.

Hudson, R. A. 1976*a*. Lexical insertion in a transformational gramm; *Foundations of Language* 12.

Hudson, R. A. 1976*b*. Conjunction-reduction, gapping, and right-noc raising. *Language* 52.

Jackendoff, R. S. 1972. *Semantic Interpretation in Generative Grammar* Cambridge: MIT Press.

Jacobs, R. A., and P. S. Rosenbaum. 1968. *English Transformational Grammar*. Waltham, Mass.: Blaisdell.

Lakoff, G. 1970*a*. Global rules. *Language* 46: 627–39.

Lakoff, G. 1970*b*. *Irregularity in Syntax*. New York: Holt, Rinehart & Winston.

Lakoff, G. 1971. On generative semantics. *Semantics: An Interdisciplinary Reader in Philosophy, Linguistics and Psychology,* ed. D. D. Steinberg and L. A. Jakobovits. London: Cambridge University Press.

Lakoff, R. 1971. Passive resistance. *Chicago Linguistic Society* 7: 149–62.

Lamb, S. M. 1964. On alternation, transformation, realization and strat-ification. *Monograph Series on Languages and Linguistics 17,* ed. J. Stu-art. Washington D.C.: Georgetown University Press.

Langacker, R. W. 1974. Movement rules in functional perspective. *Language* 50: 630–65.

Langacker, R. W. and Munro, P. 1975. Passives and their meaning. *Language* 51: 789–831.

Lasnick, H. and R. Fiengo. 1974. Complement object deletion. *Linguistic Inquiry* 5: 535–72.

Lightfoot, D. 1974. The diachronic analysis of English modals. *Montreal Working Papers in Linguistics* 3: 115–46.

McCawley, J. D. 1968*a*. Lexical insertion in a transformational grammar without deep structure. *Chicago Linguistic Society* 4: 71–80.

McCawley, J. D. 1968*b*. Concerning the base component of a transforma-tional grammar. *Foundations of Language* 4: 243–69.

McCawley, J. D. 1970. English as a VSO language. *Language* 46: 286–99.

McCawley, J. D. 1971. Tense and time reference in English. *Studies in Linguistic Semantics,* ed. C. J. Fillmore and D. T. Langendoen. New York: Holt, Rinehart & Winston.

McCord, M. C. 1975. On the form of a systemic grammar. *Journal of Linguistics* 11: 195–212.

Morgan, J. L. 1972. Verb agreement as a rule of English. *Chicago Linguistic Society* 8: 278–86.

Newmeyer, F. J. 1972. The insertion of idioms. *Chicago Linguistic Society* 8: 320–28.

Nida, E. A. 1960. *A Synopsis of English Syntax*. The Hague: Mouton.

Palmer, F. R. 1965. *A Linguistic Study of the English Verb*. London: Longman.

Parret, H. 1974. *Discussing Language*. The Hague: Mouton.

Perlmutter, D. 1971. *Deep and Surface Structure Constraints in Syntax*. New York: Holt, Rinehart & Winston.

Postal, P. M. 1966. On so-called 'pronouns' in English. *Modern Studies in English*, ed. D. A. Reibel and S. A. Schane. Englewood Cliffs, N.J.: Prentice-Hall.

Postal, P. M. 1974. *On Raising*. Cambridge: MIT Press.

Pullum, G. K. 1975. Word-order universals and grammatical relations. University College London. Mimeo.

Quirk, R., S. Greenbaum, G. Leech and J. Svartvik. 1972. *A Grammar of Contemporary English*. London: Longman.

Robinson, J. J. 1970. Dependency structures and transformational rules. *Language* 46: 259–85.

Ross, J. R. 1967. Constraints on variables in syntax. MIT Ph.D. dissertation.

Ross, J. R. 1969a. Auxiliaries as main verbs. *Studies in Philosophical Linguistics*, Series One, ed. W. Todd. Evanston, Ill.: Great Expectations.

Ross, J. R. 1969b. Guess who? *Chicago Linguistic Society* 5: 252–86.

Ross, J. R. 1970. On declarative sentences. *Readings in English Transformational Grammar*, ed. R. A. Jacobs and P. S. Rosenbaum. London: Ginn.

Ross, J. R. 1972. Doubl-ing. *Linguistic Inquiry* 3: 61–86.

Sampson, G. 1972. A proposal for constraining deletion. *Lingua* 29: 23–9.

Sampson, G. 1975. The single mother constraint. *Journal of Linguistics* 11: 1–12.

Sanders, G. A. 1970. Constraints on constituent ordering. *Papers in Linguistics* 2: 460–502.

Sanders, G. A. 1975. On the explanation of constituent order universals. *Word Order Change*, ed. C. N. Li. Austin: University of Texas Press.

Satyanarayana, P. 1973. Why saying that sentences like this are ungrammatical is wrong. *Chicago Linguistic Society* 9: 568–76.

Schachter, P. 1973. Focus and relativization. *Language* 49: 19–46.

Schachter, P. 1972. Constraints on coordination. Distributed by Indiana University Linguistics Club.

Sommerstein, A. R. 1972. On the so-called definite article in English. *Linguistic Inquiry* 3: 197–209.

Stockwell, R. P., P. Schachter and B. H. Partee. 1973. *The Major Syntactic Structures of English*. New York: Holt, Rinehart & Winston.

Tesnière, L. 1959. *Éléments de Syntaxe Structurale*. Paris: Klincksieck.

Vanek, A. L. 1970*a*. Grammatical formatives: Some basic notions. *Studies Presented to Robert P. Lees by His Students,* ed. G. Sadock and A. L. Vanek. Edmonton: Linguistic Research Inc.

Vanek, A. L. 1970*b*. *Aspects of Subject-verb Agreement*. Edmonton: University of Alberta.

Vater, H. 1975. Toward a generative dependency theory. *Lingua* 36: 121–45.

Werner, O. 1975. Von Chomsky's Aspects-modell zu einer linearen Dependenzgrammatik. *Folia Linguistica* 6: 62–88.

Winograd, T. 1972. Understanding natural language. *Cognitive Psychology* 3: 1.

Index